EXQUISITE STITCHING

WITH MULTI-HOLE BEADS

25 DELICATE DESIGNS

EXQUISITE STITCHING

WITH MULTI-HOLE BEADS

25 DELICATE DESIGNS

Renee Kovnesky

KALMBACH BOOKS

WAUKESHA, WI

Kalmbach Books
21027 Crossroads Circle
Waukesha, Wisconsin 53186
www.JewelryAndBeadingStore.com

Published in 2018
22 21 20 19 18   1 2 3 4 5

Manufactured in China

ISBN: 978-1-62700-433-6
EISBN: 978-1-62700-434-3

Editor: Erica Barse
Proofreader: Annie Pennington
Book Design: Lisa Bergman
Photographer: William Zuback

Library of Congress Control Number: 2016955348

contents

When I design and create with my favorite multi-hole beads, the resulting jewelry reminds me of beautiful Victorian-era pieces. I would have loved to wear the delicate jewels—along with the lacy, ruffled, flowing dresses (not so much the corset, though)—while walking down the steps of a castle to the ball!

projects

introduction

Different shaped beads with two, three, and four holes, OH MY!

Did you ever think we would have so many shaped beads with multiple holes for our stitching enjoyment? Me, neither! Up until a few years ago, shaped beads were rare and relatively obscure. But now, the beading world is awash in lots of different multi-hole beads—and there will be even more by the time this book is published. I have created timeless jewelry designs with some the newer and more popular older multi-hole beads.

These shaped beads can be very intimidating at first glance. You may wonder how in the world you can even begin using the bead holes. Which hole do you start with, and how do you use simple beading techniques? I've made it easy for you with straightforward illustrations and instructions.

I have organized the beads by shape and included a short description for each one. The most common two-hole seed beads, SuperDuos and MiniDuos, are incorporated into a few projects. You will also find old favorites, such as seed beads, crystals, and other multi-hole beads. You can make the projects simply by following the instructions, but I've also included some helpful stitching basics to help get you started.

I have come to love beading with these multi-hole beads, and I remain inspired by their unique shapes. They are so much fun to create with; please don't be intimated! I know once you start using these lovely shapes, you will enjoy creating beautiful jewelry with them.

— Renee

A NOTE ABOUT ILLUSTRATIONS This book is fully illustrated, with thorough instructions to help guide you through each project, step by step. Before you begin, read the short description of the featured shaped bead and how it will be used in the project.

materials

These are the materials I use and recommend.

Thread

I prefer Fireline beading thread, because I like the stiffness of the thread and the durability it provides for my finished jewelry. Use 4-lb. test, which is thin, when passing through small seed beads multiple times. Glass beads that have sharp edges, such as Czech beads or crystals, can cut thread very easily over time, so you may use 6-lb. or 8-lb. test for larger beads. A good size for most projects is 6-lb. test. It is still fine enough for 15º seed beads if you are not passing through them multiple times, and it will hold up nicely with Czech beads and crystals.

Needles

I use size 11 Tulip beading needles. I have tried many kinds of needles, and I love these needles the best. They are easy to thread, super-thin and strong, resist bending and breakage, and are very flexible and springy. They can be a little pricey, but they last a lot longer than most beading needles.

beads

Seed Beads

Not all seed beads are created equal. I like to use Miyuki and Toho, because they are manufactured with the most consistent size (except metallic seed beads, because the extra coating adds bulk). Keep this in mind when you are choosing colors. I do not recommend using Czech seed beads, which come strung on hanks, because they are very inconsistent.

Crystals

I love, love, love sparkle! I prefer Swarovski crystals, Preciosa crystals, and Thunder Polish crystals. There are some differences with these beauties that I have listed below.

Swarovski bicone crystals are the best-of-the-best quality, are consistent in size, have brilliant cuts, and offer the best selection of color choices. They can be expensive, however. Preciosa crystals are good quality, with a nice selection of color choices, and they are consistent. They are not as expensive as Swarovski crystals, but they are also not as widely available. Thunder Polish crystals are inexpensive and only available in select colors. They are not very true to size compared to the other crystals and they have very sharp edges, which can be hard on your working thread.

Multi-Hole Beads

I have chosen many of the newer and more popular multi-hole beads for my book. Some of the multi-hole beads can be substituted, so if you do not have the featured bead in a project, you might be able to use a different bead instead.

Always check all bead holes to make sure the thread will pass through each hole before you even pick it up. I keep a dressmaker headpin handy, because it is small and strong enough to help drill or poke through that closed hole.

Rectangular Beads	Round Beads	Square Beads	Triangular Beads	Other Fun Shapes
Infinity beads, Czech, 3x6mm, 2 holes	Tipp beads, Czech, 8mm, 2 holes	Tila beads, Miyuki, 5mm, 2 holes	Trinity beads, Czech, 6mm, 3 holes	Hex Pyramid beads, Czech, 12mm, 2 holes
Rulla beads, Czech, 3x5mm, 2 holes	Candy beads, Preciosa, 8mm, 2 holes	Silky beads, Czech, 6mm, 2 holes	Kheops Par Puca beads, Czech, 6mm, 2 holes	Piggy beads, Czech, 8x3.5mm, 2 holes
Bar beads, Czech-Mates, 2x6mm, 2 holes	RounDuos, Czech, 5mm, 2 holes	QuadraTile beads, CzechMates, 6mm, 4 holes	AVA beads, Czech, 10mm, 3 holes	DiamonDuos, Czech, 5x8mm, 2 holes
Super8 beads, Czech, 2.2x4.7mm, 2 holes	Honeycomb beads, Czech, 6mm, 2 holes	Tile beads, Czech-Mates, 6mm, 2 holes	Triangle beads, Czech-Mates, 6mm, 2 holes	Arcos Par Puca beads, Czech, 5x10mm, 3 hole
Half-Moon beads, CzechMates, 4x8mm, 2 holes	Cabochons, Czech-Mates, 6mm, 2 holes	Pyramid beads, Czech, 6mm, 2 holes	Tango beads, Czech, 6mm, 2 holes	Crescent beads, Czech-Mates, 10x4.5mm, 2 holes

techniques

Everyone uses different techniques for tying a knot and for ending and adding threads. I will explain a few of my techniques that work the best for me. If you already have a favorite knot or a great way to end or add a new thread, please feel free to use your own technique. Stick with the technique that work best for you.

Surgeon's Knot

To make a surgeon's knot, bring the left thread over and around the right thread twice. Bring the right thread over and around the left thread one time and pull to tighten.

Half-Hitch Knot

Pass the needle under the thread bridge between to beads, and pull gently until a loop forms. Pass through the loop, and pull gently to draw the knot into the beadwork.

Adding Thread

To add a thread, pass into the beadwork a few rows behind the point where the last bead was added, leaving about a 2-in. (5cm) tail. Follow the same thread path of the stitch. Tie a half-hitch knot between a few beads as you pass to where you will continue with your project. Cut the tail from the added thread.

Ending Thread

To end a thread, pass back through a few beads into your project, and tie a half-hitch knot. Pass back through a few more beads, tie another half-hitch knot, pass through a few more beads, and cut the thread.

Stop Bead

A stop bead is used to temporary secure the beads to begin some stitching projects. Choose a bead that is different from the ones you are using, so you don't get confused that it may be part of your project. Pick up the stop bead, leaving the desired length tail. Pass through the stop bead again in the same direction. You may pass through the stop bead one more time for added security.

Opening and Closing Jump Rings

Jump rings are added to connect chain and extenders together and to connect the chain and clasps together to complete the project.

1. Hold the jump ring with two pairs of flatnose or chainnose pliers.

2. To open the jump ring, bring the tips of one pair of pliers towards you, and the tips of the other pair of pliers away from you. To close the jump ring, bring the tips of one pair of pliers away from you, and the other pair of pliers toward you.

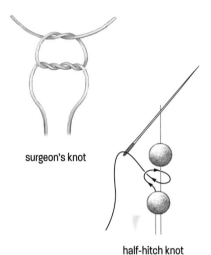

surgeon's knot

half-hitch knot

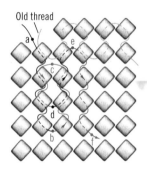

Old thread

adding and ending thread

stop bead

stitches

My favorite stitch is the picot. A picot stitch gives a delicate Victorian, lacy look to your finished jewelry. You will find that I have incorporated this stitch in almost all of my designs. I have listed a few common stitches that are used frequently throughout the book.

Picot

1. Exit a bead, and pick up three beads (**figure 1, red path**).
2. Make a circle by passing back through the first bead in the same direction, then through the indicated beads (**blue path**).

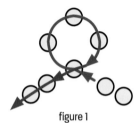

figure 1

Picot Points

1. Pass through the base bead and up through the side bead of the existing picot (**figure 2, red path**).
2. Skip the next bead, and then pass down through the next side bead and the base bead in the same direction (**green path**).
3. If the bead you skipped is not pointing outward, take your needle and pull the bead outward to help create the point.

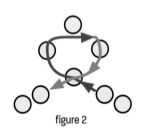

figure 2

Right-Angle Weave

1. Pick up four beads, pass back through all the beads one more time, and tie a surgeon's knot (**figure 3, blue path**). Sew through three beads (**red path**).
2. Pick up three beads, pass back through the last bead in the previous circle (**figure 4, green path**), and sew through two beads (**orange path**).
3. You will be going in the opposite direction as you make each right-angle weave three-bead stitch. Continue adding each right-angle weave stitch for the desired length.

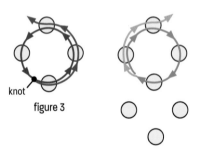

knot

figure 3

figure 4

1 rectangular beads

dancing
angels
necklace

Make a dainty necklace, perfect for a special outfit. This piece is made with Matubo Rulla beads, which are rectangular with rounded corners and two holes.

top hole
bottom hole

WORKING WITH RULLA BEADS

Rulla beads have rounded corners with two holes. Before you begin, lay the beads out on the beading mat, all facing the same direction. The instructions will indicate which hole to sew through: top or bottom.

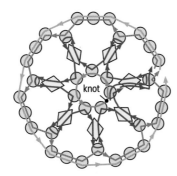

knot

figure 1

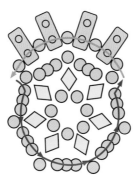

figure 2

supplies

Necklace, 16 in. (41cm)

- **25** Rulla beads
- **34** 4mm Swarovski bicone crystals
- 3g 11º seed beads
- 20 in. (51cm) 3mm rolo chain
- 3 in. (7.6cm) chain extender (optional)
- **2** 5mm jump rings
- lobster claw clasp
- Fireline, 6-lb. test
- beading needle, size 11
- scissors and **2** pairs of pliers

make the heptagon

1. Thread a needle on 1½ yd. (1.4m) of thread, leaving a 3-in. (7.6cm) tail. Keep a tight tension as you work. Pick up seven 11º seed beads, and sew through all the beads again to make a circle. Tie a surgeon's knot (Techniques, p. 9) **(figure 1, green path)**.

2. Sew through the next 11º, pick up a 4mm crystal and an 11º, and sew back through the crystal and the next 11º. Repeat around the circle **(red path)**.

3. Sew through the next crystal and 11º **(blue path)**.

4. Pick up three 11ºs, and sew through the next 11º. Repeat around the circle **(pink path)**.

5. Repeat step 4, but skip the 11ºs that are above the crystals (when skipping the 11ºs, the thread will lie behind the 11ºs). Repeat around the component, pulling the thread tight, until it forms a heptagon shape. Exit an end 11º in a group of three 11ºs. You will notice the 11ºs above the crystals will be pushed up and the three 11ºs will lie below **(orange path)**.

add the first row of Rulla beads

1. Pick up a repeating pattern of an 11º and a Rulla bead (bottom hole) four times, and then pick up an 11º **(figure 2, orange path)**.

2. Skip the next two groups of three 11ºs, and sew through the next five groups of three 11ºs on the outside of the component **(red path)**.

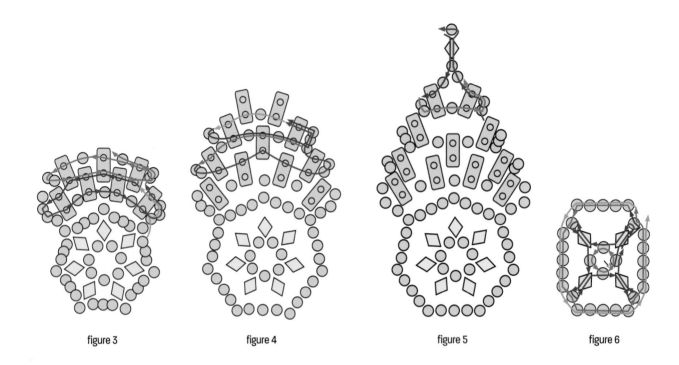

figure 3 figure 4 figure 5 figure 6

add the second row of Rullas

1. Skip the 11º above the crystal, sew through an 11º next to the Rulla, pick up two 11ºs, and sew through a Rulla (top hole) **(figure 3, orange path)**.

2. Pick up a Rulla, and sew through the following Rulla (top hole). Repeat this stitch twice **(blue path)**.

3. Pick up two 11ºs, and sew through a Rulla (bottom hole) and an 11º three times. Continue through a Rulla (bottom hole) three 11ºs, and a Rulla (top hole) **(red path)**.

4. Pick up two 11ºs, sew through the next Rulla (top hole), pick up an 11º, sew through a Rulla (top hole), pick up an 11º, and sew through a Rulla (top hole) **(pink path)**.

5. Pick up two 11ºs, and sew through the following beads: a Rulla (bottom hole), a Rulla (top hole), a Rulla (bottom hole), a Rulla (top hole), a Rulla (bottom hole), two 11ºs, a Rulla (top hole), and an 11º **(green path)**.

add the third and fourth row of Rullas

1. Pick up a Rulla and an 11º, and sew through a Rulla (top hole). Pick up an 11º, a Rulla, and an 11º, and sew through a Rulla (top hole) **(figure 4, green path)**.

2. Sew back through two 11ºs, a Rulla (bottom hole), a Rulla (top hole), a Rulla (bottom hole), a Rulla (top hole), a Rulla (bottom hole), two 11ºs, a Rulla (top hole), and an 11º, and pick up two 11ºs. Continue through a Rulla (top hole) **(red path)**.

3. Pick up a Rulla, an 11º, and a Rulla, and sew through a Rulla (top hole) **(orange path)**.

4. Pick up two 11ºs, and sew through a Rulla (bottom hole), an 11º, a Rulla (top hole), an 11º, a Rulla (bottom hole), three 11ºs, and a Rulla (top hole) **(blue path)**.

add a drop to the component

1. Pick up two 11ºs, sew through a Rulla (top hole), and pick up two 11ºs, a crystal, and an 11º **(figure 5, red path)**.

2. Sew back through the crystal and the next 11º, then pick up an 11º, and sew through a Rulla (top hole) **(blue path)**.

3. Pick up two 11ºs, and sew through a Rulla (bottom hole), an 11º, a Rulla (bottom hole), two 11ºs, and a Rulla (top hole) **(green path)**.

4. Retrace the thread path, sewing through the beads again to secure. End the threads (Techniques).

make the small components

1. Cut about 1½ yd. (1.4m) of thread for the new component, and thread a needle on one end. Keep a tight tension. Pick up four 11ºs, and sew through all the beads again to make a circle. Leave about a 3-in. tail. Tie a surgeon's knot **(figure 6, green path)**.

2. Sew through the next 11º, pick up a crystal and an 11º, and sew back through the crystal and the next 11º. Repeat around the circle **(red path)**.

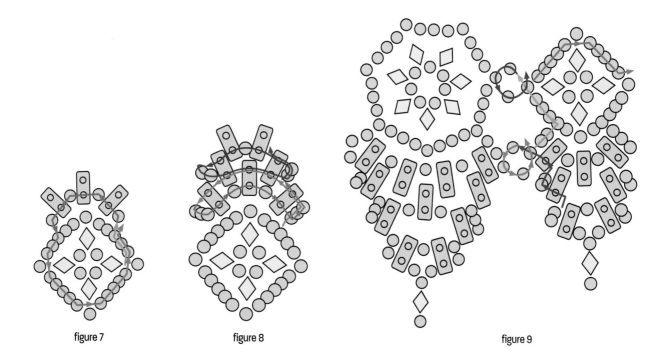

figure 7

figure 8

figure 9

3. Sew through a crystal and an 11º. End the tail (**blue path**).

4. Pick up five 11ºs, and sew through the next 11º. Repeat around the circle (**pink path**).

5. Repeat step 4, but skip the 11ºs above the crystals (the thread should lie behind the 11ºs). Pull tight until the component is a nice, square shape (**orange path**).

add the first row of Rullas

1. Skip the 11º above the crystal, and sew through the next three 11ºs (**figure 7, orange path**).

2. Pick up a repeating pattern of an 11º and a Rulla three times, and then pick up an 11º (**pink path**).

3. Skip the next five 11ºs, including the 11º above the crystals, and sew through the next 16 11ºs on the outside of the component, skipping the 11º above the crystals (**green path**).

add the second and third rows of Rullas

1. Sew through the 11º next to the Rulla. Pick up two 11ºs, and sew through a Rulla (top hole). Pick up a Rulla, and sew through a Rulla (top hole). Pick up a Rulla, and sew through a Rulla (top hole) (**figure 8, green path**).

2. Pick up two 11ºs, and sew through an 11º, a Rulla (bottom hole), an 11º, a Rulla (bottom hole), an 11º, a Rulla (bottom hole), three 11ºs, and a Rulla (top hole) (**pink path**).

3. Pick up two 11ºs, and sew through a Rulla (top hole). Pick up a Rulla, an 11º, and a Rulla, and sew through a Rulla (top hole) (**blue path**).

4. Pick up two 11ºs, and sew through a Rulla (bottom hole), a Rulla (top hole), a Rulla (bottom hole), two 11ºs, and a Rulla (top hole) (**red path**).

5. Follow the steps on p. 14 to add a drop to the component. End the tail only (leave the working thread).

6. Make a second small component.

connect the components

NOTE: When connecting the components, make sure they are facing the same way.

1. Use the working thread of a small component: Exit the top hole of a Rulla as shown, and sew through a Rulla (top hole), two 11ºs, a Rulla (top hole), and an 11º (**figure 9, red path**).

2. Pick up an 11º, and sew through the first 11º on the end of the large component in the first row of Rullas. Pick up an 11º, and sew back through the 11º in the small component you first exited in the same direction. Retrace the thread path through these four beads to secure the connection (**green path**).

3. Sew through two 11ºs next to the Rullas and five 11ºs on the outer edge of the component, exiting the protruding 11º (**orange path**).

4. Pick up a 11º, and sew through the middle protruding 11º on the outer edge

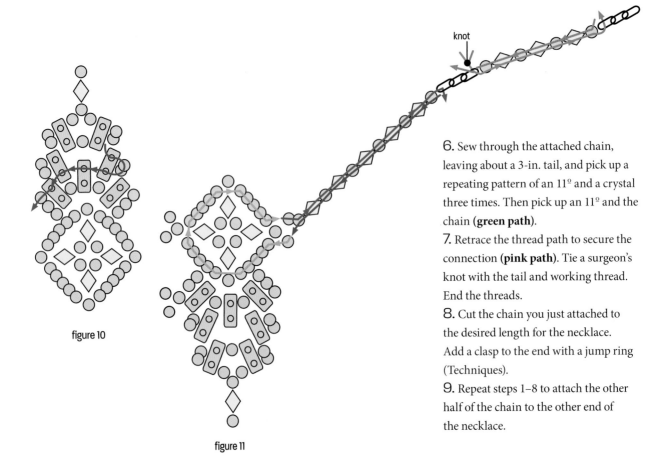

figure 10

figure 11

6. Sew through the attached chain, leaving about a 3-in. tail, and pick up a repeating pattern of an 11º and a crystal three times. Then pick up an 11º and the chain (**green path**).

7. Retrace the thread path to secure the connection (**pink path**). Tie a surgeon's knot with the tail and working thread. End the threads.

8. Cut the chain you just attached to the desired length for the necklace. Add a clasp to the end with a jump ring (Techniques).

9. Repeat steps 1–8 to attach the other half of the chain to the other end of the necklace.

of the larger component. Pick up an 11º, and sew back through the 11º in the small component you just exited in the same direction. Retrace the thread path through these four beads to secure the connection (**blue path**).

5. Sew through five 11ºs on the outer edge, skip an 11º, and sew through the next five 11ºs on the outer edge. Leave the working thread (**pink path**).

6. Use the working thread of the second small component: Sew through the next Rulla (top hole), two 11ºs, Rulla (bottom hole), Rulla (top hole), Rulla (bottom hole), Rulla (top hole), and 11º (**figure 10, red path**).

7. Repeat steps 1–5 to complete the connection (you will be going in the opposite direction).

attach the chain

1. Exit an 11º in the small component, and pick up two 11ºs and a repeating pattern of a crystal and an 11º five times. Then, pick up the chain (**figure 11, red path**).

2. Sew back through an 11º and a crystal a total of five times, and then sew through an 11º (**blue path**).

3. Pick up an 11º, and sew back through 20 11ºs on the outer edge of the small component (skipping the 11ºs above the crystals) (**orange path**).

4. Retrace the thread path to secure the connection. End the threads.

5. Cut about 1 in. (2.5cm) off the chain you just attached. Attach a new thread about 1 yd. (.9m) long.

garden path
bracelet

Make a timeless treasure with this lovely, lacy piece. This bracelet is stitched with Czech Infinity beads, which are in the shape of an infinity symbol, or figure-eight.

supplies

Bracelet, 8 in. (20cm)

- 4g Infinity beads
- 5g MiniDuos
- **80** 3mm bicone crystals
- 2g 11º seed beads
- 3g 15º seed beads
- 13mm ball-and-socket clasp
- Fireline, 6-lb. test
- beading needle, size 11

start the bracelet

1. Thread a needle on 2 yd. (1.8m) of thread, leaving about a 3-in. (7.6cm) tail. Pick up two 11ºs seed beads and two Infinity beads, and sew down through the same two Infinitys (empty holes). Pick up an 11º. Tie a surgeon's knot **(figure 1, red path)** (Techniques, p. 9).

2. Sew through two 11ºs and two Infinitys (right holes). Pick up an Infinity, and end the tail **(green path)** (Techniques).

3. Pick up an 11º, a 3mm bicone crystal, an 11º, and three Infinitys. Repeat for the desired length of the bracelet, leaving about an inch for the clasp. End with three Infinitys **(blue path)**.

4. Pick up three 11ºs, and sew down through three Infinitys (empty holes) **(orange path)**.

5. Pick up an 11º, a crystal, and an 11º, and sew down through three Infinitys (empty holes). Repeat until you exit the last three Infinitys at the end of the bracelet **(pink path)**.

continue the bracelet

1. Sew through three 11ºs and three Infinitys (right holes) **(figure 2, green path)**.

2. Pick up three MiniDuos, sew through two Infinitys (right holes), and pick up

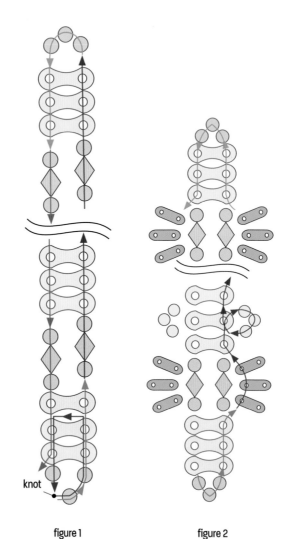

figure 1

figure 2

three 15ºs **(red path)**.

3. Make a picot by sewing back through the Infinity you are currently exiting and then the next Infinity **(blue path)** (Techniques).

4. Repeat steps 2 and 3 to the end of the bracelet.

5. When you reach the last three Infinitys, continue through those Infinitys (right holes), three 11ºs, and the next three Infinitys (left holes) on the other side of the bracelet **(orange path)**.

6. Repeat step 2–5 on the other side of the bracelet.

left hole   right hole

WORKING WITH INFINITY BEADS

Infinity beads are shaped like a figure-eight with two holes. Before you begin, lay the beads out on a beading mat, all facing the same direction. The instructions will indicate which hole to sew through: left, right, or empty.

embellish the bracelet

1. Sew through a MiniDuo (empty hole). Pick up a crystal, and sew through the next MiniDuo (empty hole). Pick up a crystal, and sew through the next MiniDuo (empty hole) **(figure 3, red path)**.

2. Secure the picot by sewing down through the bottom 15º, up through the next 15º, and then through the side 15º **(green path)**.

3. Sew back down through the bottom 15º and up through the next 15º **(orange path)**.

4. Repeat step 1–3 until you reach the the end of the bracelet, ending with step 3.

5. Sew up through a MiniDuo (empty hole), pick up a crystal, sew through a MiniDuo (outer hole), pick up a crystal, and sew through a MiniDuo (empty hole). Sew through three Infinitys (right holes), three 11ºs, and three Infinitys (left holes) **(blue path)**.

6. Repeat steps 1–5. In step 5, sew through only the last two Infinitys (right holes) at the end **(purple path)**.

embellish and add the clasp

1. Exit the Infinity, and pick up a 15º **(figure 4, purple path)**.

2. Sew through a MiniDuo (outer hole) and a crystal, pick up three 15ºs, and sew through a crystal and a MiniDuo (outer hole) **(red path)**.

3. Pick up two 15ºs, and sew through the middle 15º of the picot. Pick up two 15ºs **(orange path)**.

4. Repeat steps 2 and 3 to the end of the bracelet, ending with step 2.

5. Exit a MiniDuo, pick up a 15º, and sew through two Infinitys (right holes) and two 11ºs **(green path)**.

6. Pick up two 11ºs and the clasp **(blue path)**.

7. Sew down through the 11º just picked up, pick up an 11º, and sew back through the middle 11º **(pink path)**.

8. Retrace the thread path to secure the connection.

9. Pick up an 11º and sew through two Infinitys (left holes). Pick up a 15º (for the first end only; for the second end, sew through the 15º instead of picking one up) **(gray path)**. Repeat steps 1–9 on the other end of the bracelet. End the thread.

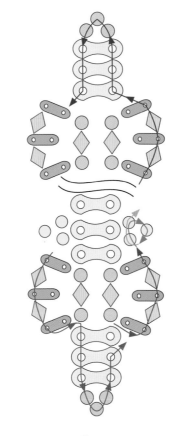

figure 3

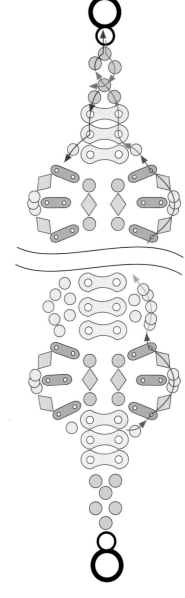

figure 4

sparkling
wings
bracelet

I love how a certain shape can result in surprising effects—like in this bracelet. Flat Bar beads create fan-like shapes.

WORKING WITH BAR BEADS

Bar beads are flat, slightly oval-shaped beads with two holes. Lay the beads out on the beading mat all facing the same direction. The instructions will indicate which hole to sew through: top, bottom, or empty.

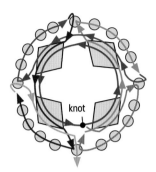

knot

figure 1

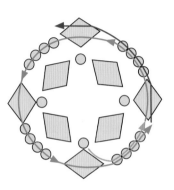

figure 2

make the components

1. Thread a needle on 1½ yd. (1.4m) of thread, leaving a 4-in. (10cm) tail. Pick up four 3mm crystals, and make a circle by sewing through all the beads again. Tie a surgeon's knot (**figure 1, blue path**) (Techniques, p. 9). Exit by the knot.

2. Sew through a crystal, and pick up six 15º seed beads (**pink path**).

3. Sew back through the crystal (the 15ºs that were just added will lie on top of the first crystal). Continue through a crystal, and pick up five 15ºs (**green path**).

4. Sew down through the next 15º, sew through two crystals, and pick up five 15ºs (**red path**). Sew down through the next 15º, sew through two crystals, sew up through the next 15º, and pick up four 15º (**gray path**). Sew down through the next 15º and a crystal, and sew up through the next 15º (**orange path**). End the tail (Techniques).

add crystals

1. Sew through four 15ºs (**figure 2, orange path**).

2. Pick up a crystal, and sew through four 15ºs. Repeat three times (**green path**).

3. Sew through a crystal, four 15ºs, and a crystal (**red path**).

continue to embellish

1. Pick up a 15º, three Bar beads, and a 15º. Sew back through the crystal to secure (**figure 3, orange path**).

2. Sew through the next 15º, pick up four 15ºs, and sew through a Bar (empty hole). Pick up a crystal and four 15ºs (**green path**).

3. Sew back through the crystal (the four 15ºs will lie on top of the crystal) and a Bar (empty hole). Pick up a crystal and four 15ºs (**pink path**).

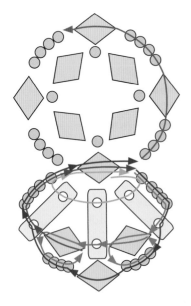

figure 3

4. Sew back through the crystal and a Bar (empty hole). Pick up four 15⁰s, and sew through a 15⁰ and a crystal (**red path**).

5. Sew through five 15⁰s, a Bar, and four 15⁰s. Pick up a crystal (see Note below), and sew through four 15⁰s, a Bar, five 15⁰s, and a crystal (**blue path**). Retrace the thread path to secure the last crystal.

6. Sew through the next four 15⁰s, a crystal, four 15⁰s, and a crystal (**purple path**).

7. Repeat steps 1–6 to complete the other side of the component. Weave the working thread through the beads until you exit the end crystal. Do not end the working thread.

NOTE: If you are using Thunder Polish 3mm bicones or 3x2mm rondelles, you will probably need to add a 15⁰ before and after the crystal added in step 5 to fill the space.

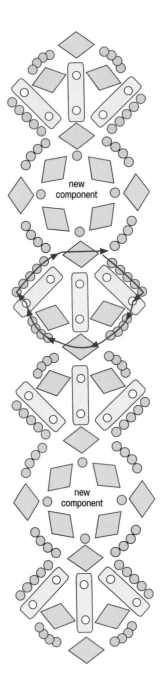

figure 4

figure 5

make and connect a new component

1. Thread a needle on 1½ yd. (1.4m) of thread, leaving a 4-in. (10cm) tail. Repeat the instructions up to step 7 of "Continue to Embellish," p. 21.

2. Follow step 7, but instead of picking up a crystal in step 5, sew through the existing crystal at the end of the completed component, and continue with steps 5 and 6 (**figure 4, blue path**). End the thread.

3. Repeat for all other components to the desired length, leaving room for the clasp. After adding the last component, sew through the piece to exit the end crystal.

add the clasp

1. Use the working thread from the end component: Pick up three 15⁰s and one half of the clasp (**figure 5, green path**).

2. Sew back down through the 15⁰ below the clasp, pick up two 15⁰s, and sew through the end crystal (**blue path**). Retrace the thread path to reinforce the connection, and end the thread.

3. Repeat to add the other half of the clasp to the other end of the bracelet.

crossed stars
bracelet

Super8 beads are a delicate version of a double-hole bead in—you guessed it—the shape of an eight. They're perfect for a pretty bracelet that will go with anything.

supplies

Bracelet, 8 in. (20cm)

- 8g Super8 beads
- **32** 3mm crystal cubes
- 1g 11º seed beads
- 3g 15º seed beads
- ball-and-socket clasp
- Fireline, 4-lb. test
- beading needle, size 11

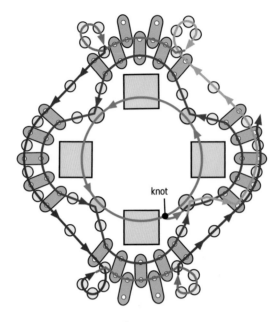

figure 1

make the first component

1. Thread a needle on 1 yd. (.9m) of thread, leaving a 4-in. (10cm) tail. Pick up a repeating pattern of an 11º seed bead and a crystal cube bead a total of four times. Make a circle by sewing back through all the beads again. Tie a surgeon's knot **(figure 1, green path)** (Techniques, p. 9).

2. Sew through an 11º, and pick up a 15º seed bead, five Super8s, and a 15º. Repeat around the circle. End the tail **(red path)** (Techniques).

3. Sew through an 11º, a 15º, and a Super8 (empty hole), pick up a 15º, and sew through a Super8 (empty hole). Pick up a 15º, and sew through a Super8 (empty hole) three more times. Then pick up a 15º, sew through a Super8 (empty hole), and pick up four 15ºs **(orange path)**.

4. Make a picot by sewing back through the first 15º, and then sew through a Super8 (empty hole). Pick up a Super8, sew through a Super8 (empty hole), pick up a Super8, and sew through a Super8 (empty hole). Then, pick up four 15ºs **(pink path)**.

5. Make a picot by sewing back through the first 15º (Techniques), and then sew through the next Super8 (empty hole).

Pick up a 15º, sew through a Super8 (empty hole), pick up a 15º, and sew through a Super8 (empty hole). Pick up a 15º, and sew through a Super8 (empty hole) three more times. Then, pick up a 15º, sew through a Super8 (empty hole), and pick up four 15ºs **(blue path)**.

6. Make a picot by sewing back through the first 15º, and then sew through the next Super8 (empty hole). Pick up a Super8, and sew through a Super8 (empty hole). Pick up a Super8, and sew through a Super8 (empty hole). Then, pick up four 15ºs **(pink path)**.

7. Make a picot by sewing back through the first 15º, and then sew through the next Super8 **(gray path)**. Do not end the working thread.

make and connect more components

1. Repeat steps 1–5 of "Make the First Component."

2. Make a picot by sewing back through the first 15º, and then sew through the next Super8 (empty hole). Sew through a Super8 (empty hole) in the completed

top hole

bottom hole

WORKING WITH SUPER8 BEADS
Czech Super8 beads have a delicate slim waist, in the shape of a figure-eight, with two holes. Lay the beads out on the beading mat facing the same direction. The instructions will indicate which hole to sew through: top, bottom, and empty.

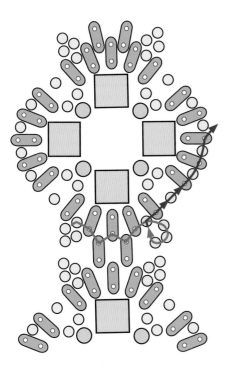

figure 2

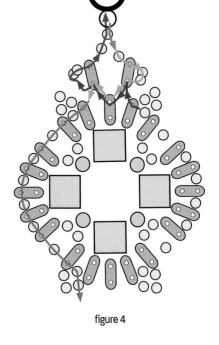

figure 4

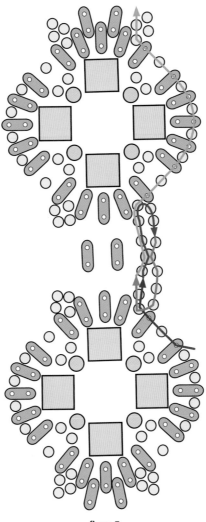

figure 3

component, a Super8 (empty hole) in the uncompleted component, a Super8 (empty hole) in the completed component, and a Super8 (empty hole) in the uncompleted component. Pick up four 15°s (**figure 2, pink path**).

3. Make a picot by sewing back through the first 15°, and then sew through the next Super8 (empty hole) in the uncompleted component. Pick up a 15° and sew through a few beads in the uncompleted component, tie a half-hitch knot, and end the thread (**blue path**).

4. Repeat steps 1–3 for the desired length of the bracelet.

embellish the sides

1. Thread a needle on 2 yd. (1.8m) of thread, leaving a 4-in. (10cm) tail. Sew through the fifth outer edge Super8 of the first component. Tie a half-hitch knot, and sew through a 15°, a Super8, and two 15°s in the picot (**figure 3, blue path**).

2. Pick up a 15°, an 11°, and a 15°, and sew through the next four 15°s in the picot of the next component (**red path**).

3. Pick up a 15°, sew through an 11°, pick up a 15°, and sew through the four 15°s in the picot of the previous component (**green path**).

4. Sew through a 15°, an 11°, and three 15°s, and continue through a Super8 and a 15° a total of seven times on the outer edge of the component. Then sew through a 15° in the picot (**orange path**).

5. Repeat steps 2–4 to complete this side of the bracelet. Don't sew through the 15° in the picot of the very last component.

add the clasp

1. Exit a 15°, and sew through a Super8 (top hole), a Super8 (bottom hole), a Super8 (top hole), and a Super8 (bottom hole) (**figure 4, blue path**).

2. Pick up two 15°s, sew up through a Super8 (top hole), and pick up two 15°s and the clasp (**red path**). Sew back down through the 15° below the clasp (**green path**).

3. Pick up a 15°, and sew through a Super8 (top hole). Pick up two 15°s, and sew down through a Super8 (bottom hole), a Super8 (top hole) and a Super8 (bottom hole) (**orange path**). Sew through all the beads a few times to secure the clasp.

4. Sew through a Super8 and a 15° a total of eight times on the outer side of the component, and then sew through a 15° (**pink path**).

5. Repeat "Embellish the Sides," steps 2–5, and "Add the Clasp," steps 1–4 to complete the bracelet. End the thread.

moonshine
earrings

Half-Moon two-hole beads are cleverly designed to mimic a familiar shape. You only need a handful to make this beautiful pair of earrings.

left right
hole hole

**WORKING
WITH
HALF-MOON
BEADS**

The top of a
Half-Moon
bead is domed,
and the bottom
is flat. It is
important to
pick up the
bead through
the correct
hole. Lay the
beads on
your beading
mat with the
domed side
facing up. The
instructions
will indicate
which hole to
sew through:
right or left.

supplies

- **10** Half-Moon beads
- **32** 2x3mm fire-polished rondelles
- 1g 11º seed beads
- 2g 15º seed beads
- **2** 12x6mm teardrops
- pair of earring findings
- Fireline, 6-lb. test
- beading needle, size 11

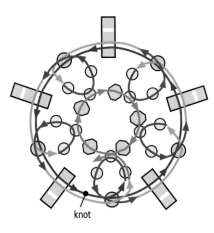

knot

figure 1

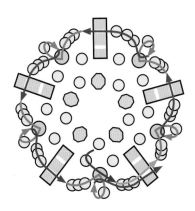

figure 2

start the component

1. Thread a needle on 2 yd. (1.8m) of thread, leaving a 4-in. (10cm) tail. Pick up an 11º seed bead and a Half-Moon bead (left hole) five times. Sew back through all the beads one more time, tie a surgeon's knot, and sew through an 11º (**figure 1, blue path**) (Techniques, p. 9).

2. Pick up three 15º seed beads, and sew back through the 11º in the same direction (**red path**). Sew through a Half-Moon (left hole) and an 11º (**orange path**). Repeat this step around the circle to make a total of five picots (Techniques).

3. Sew through two 15ºs to exit the middle 15º in a picot. Pick up a rondelle

and sew through the next middle 15º in a picot. Repeat around the inner circle (**green path**).

embellish

1. Sew through a 15º and an 11º (**figure 2, blue path**). Pick up three 15ºs, and sew through a Half-Moon (right hole) (**orange path**).

2. Pick up three 15ºs, sew through an 11º, and pick up a 15º (**green path**).

3. Sew back through the 11º in the same direction. Pick up three 15ºs, and sew through a Half-Moon (right hole) (**red path**).

4. Repeat steps 2 and 3 around the circle.

finish the earring

1. Exit a Half-Moon (right hole), and pick up a 15°, a rondelle, three 15°s, a rondelle, and a 15°, and sew through a Half-Moon (right hole). Repeat around the circle **(figure 3, red path)**.

2. Exit a Half-Moon (right hole), and sew through a 15°, a rondelle, and a 15°. Skip a 15°, and sew through a 15°, a rondelle, a 15°, a Half-Moon (right hole), a 15°, a rondelle, and two 15°s **(green path)**.

3. Pick up a rondelle, five 15°s, an earring finding, and four 15°s **(pink path)**. Sew back through the first 15° picked up, in the same direction, a rondelle, two 15°s, a rondelle, a 15°, and a Half-Moon (right hole) **(teal path)**.

4. Sew through a 15°, a rondelle, and a 15°. Skip a 15°, and sew through a 15°, a rondelle, a 15°, a Half-Moon (right hole), a 15°, a rondelle, and a 15°. Skip a 15°, and sew through a 15° and a rondelle **(orange path)**.

5. Pick up nine 15°s, a teardrop, and four 15°s, and sew back up through the fifth 15° from the first 15° **(blue path)**.

6. Pick up four 15°s, and sew up through a rondelle and a 15°. Skip a 15°, and sew up through a 15°, a rondelle, a 15°, and a Half-Moon (right hole) **(black path)**. Retrace the thread path to reinforce the connection, and end the threads (Techniques).

7. Repeat to make a second earring.

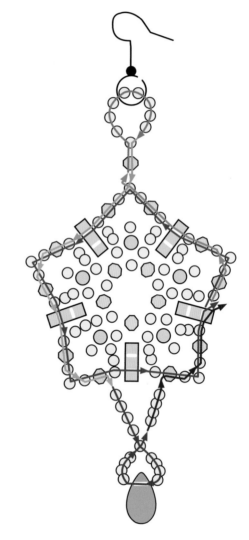

figure 3

2 round beads

quilted
pendant

A tassel brightens up any outfit, and this pendant, made using Czech Tipp two-hole beads, is no exception. A Tipp bead is shaped like a small cone (or chocolate chip) with two holes that run through the base of the bead—perfect for a statement piece!

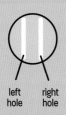

left
hole

right
hole

**WORKING
WITH TIPP
BEADS**

Tipp beads
have a pointed
top and a flat
bottom. The
illustrations
show a flat
bead, so it is
very important
to sew through
the correct
hole. Lay the
Tipp beads
on your bead-
ing mat with the
pointed side
facing up. The
instructions will
indicate which
hole to sew or
pass through:
right, left,
inside, outside,
or top.

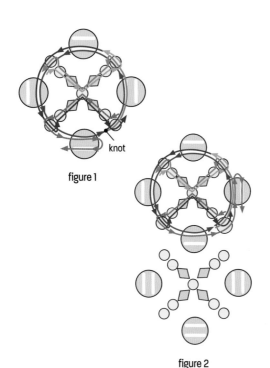

knot

figure 1

figure 2

supplies

- **12** 8mm Tipp beads
- **18** 4mm bicone crystals
- 3g 11º seed beads
- 8.5x9.5mm (or similar size) bead cap
- 4½ ft. (1.4m) 5.5mm fine cable chain
- **2** 5mm jump rings
- lobster claw clasp
- Fireline, 6 lb. test
- beading needles, #12
- wire cutters

start the component

1. Thread a needle on 2 yd. (1.8m) of thread, leaving about a 3-in. (7.6cm) tail.
2. Pick up an 11º seed bead and a Tipp bead (left hole) a total of four times. Make a circle by passing back through all the beads again, and tie a surgeon's knot **(figure 1, red path)** (Techniques, p. 9).
3. Sew through an 11º, a Tipp (inside hole), and an 11º, and pick up an 11º, a 4mm bicone crystal, an 11º, a crystal, and an 11º. Pass through the adjacent 11º **(green path)**.
4. Sew back through an 11º, a crystal, an 11º, a crystal, and two 11ºs **(orange path)**.
5. Sew through a Tipp (inside hole), an 11º, a Tipp (inside hole), and an 11º, pick up an 11º and a crystal, and sew through the middle 11º. Pick up a crystal and an 11º, and sew through the adjacent 11º **(blue path)**.

6. Sew back through an 11º, a crystal, an 11º, a crystal, two 11ºs, and a Tipp (inside hole), and sew up through the same Tipp (outside hole) in the opposite direction **(pink path)**. Rotate the beadwork 180 degrees.

make the second square

1. Pick up an 11º, a Tipp (left hole), an 11º, a Tipp (left hole), an 11º, a Tipp (left hole), and an 11º. Sew through the inside hole of the Tipp on the current component you are adding **(figure 2, red path)**.
2. Sew through an 11º, a Tipp (inside hole), and an 11º, and pick up an 11º, a crystal, an 11º, a crystal, and an 11º. Sew through the adjacent 11º **(green path)**.
3. Sew back through an 11º, a crystal, an 11º, a crystal, and two 11ºs **(orange path)**.
4. Sew through a Tipp (inside hole), an 11º, a Tipp (inside hole), and an 11º, and pick up an 11º and a crystal. Sew through

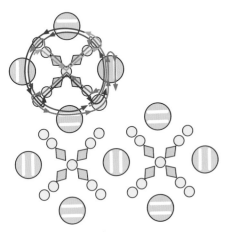

figure 3

the middle 11º, pick up a crystal and an 11º, and sew through the adjacent 11º **(blue path)**.

5. Sew back through an 11º, a crystal, an 11º, a crystal, two 11ºs, a Tipp (inside hole), an 11º, and a Tipp (inside hole), and sew up through the same Tipp (inside hole) in the opposite direction **(pink path)**.

6. Repeat steps 1–5 to make another component **(figure 3)**.

make the final square

1. Pick up an 11º, and sew through a Tipp (outside hole) on the first square. Pick up an 11º, a Tipp (left hole), an 11º, a Tipp (left hole), and an 11º, and sew through the Tipp on the inside hole of the component you are adding **(figure 4, red path)**.

2. Sew through an 11º, a Tipp (inside hole), and an 11º, and pick up an 11º, a crystal, an 11º, a crystal, and an 11º. Sew through the adjacent 11º **(green path)**.

3. Sew back through an 11º, a crystal, an 11º, a crystal, and two 11ºs **(orange path)**.

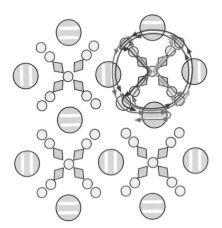

figure 4

4. Sew through a Tipp (inside hole), an 11º, a Tipp (inside hole), and an 11º, and pick up an 11º and a crystal. Sew through the middle 11º, pick up a crystal and an 11º, and sew through the adjacent 11º **(blue path)**.

5. Sew back through an 11º, a crystal, an 11º, a crystal, two 11ºs, a Tipp (inside hole), an 11º, and a Tipp (inside hole). Sew up through the same Tipp (outside hole of the fourth component) in the opposite direction **(pink path)**.

connect the squares

1. Sew through an 11º in the first square. Pick up an 11º, and sew through an 11º in the second square. Pick up an 11º, and sew through an 11º in the third square. Pick up an 11º, and sew through an 11º in the fourth square. Pick up an 11º, and sew back through an 11º in the first square **(figure 5, blue path)**.

2. Sew back through the next 11º that was added in the previous step. Skip the next 11º in the square. Repeat around the circle **(red path)**.

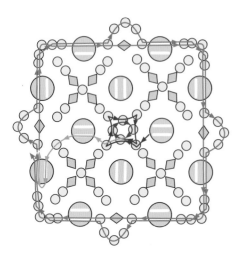

figure 5

figure 6

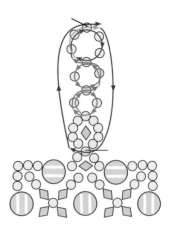

figure 7

3. Sew through two 11ºs, a Tipp on the second square (inside hole), an 11º, and a Tipp on the second square (inside hole). Sew through the same Tipp (outside hole of the second component) in the opposite direction (**orange path**).

4. Pick up an 11º, a crystal, and an 11º. Sew through a Tipp (outside hole), pick up five 11ºs, and sew through a Tipp (outside hole). Repeat around the component (**green path**).

5. Sew through an 11º, pick up three 11ºs, and sew through an 11º, a Tipp (outside hole), and two 11ºs. Skip an 11º, and sew through two 11ºs and a Tipp (outside hole). Repeat around the component (**pink path**).

make the bail

1. Sew through three 11ºs, and pick up a crystal and an 11º (**figure 6, blue path**).

figure 8

2. Sew back through the crystal and 11º in the same direction (**orange path**).

3. Pick up four 11ºs, sew through the 11º above the crystal, pick up four 11ºs, and sew through the 11º you originally exited in the same direction (**green path**).

4. Sew through the next five 11ºs to exit the 11º above the crystal (**red path**).

finish the bail

1. Pick up three 11ºs, and make a circle by sewing back through the 11º just exited in the same direction. Retrace the thread path to reinforce the circle (**figure 7, green path**).

2. Sew through the next two 11ºs (**pink path**).

3. Repeat steps 1 and 2 to make another circle.

4. Pick up five 11ºs, and make a circle by sewing back through the 11º just exited in the same direction. Retrace the thread path to reinforce the circle (**red path**).

5. Sew through the next three 11ºs (**orange path**).

6. Fold the bail in half. Flip the pendant over so the back is facing you.

7. Sew through the middle base 11º in the same direction (**blue path**).

8. Sew back through the middle top 11º in the same direction you are exiting the middle base 11º (**gray path**). Retrace the thread path to reinforce the connection.

Back of pendant

add the tassel

1. Cut 10–15 2-in. (5cm) pieces of chain. (You may have to cut these pieces shorter or longer, depending on the size and length of your bead cap.)

2. Sew through the beadwork as shown to exit the bottom 11º (**figure 8, blue path**).

3. Pick up a crystal, a bead cap (small end first), and the chain pieces (**red path**).

4. Sew back up through the bead cap, crystal, and 11º in the same direction. Pull the chain tight into the bead cap (**green path**).

5. End the threads (Techniques). Add the desired length of chain to the pendant, and attach jump rings and a clasp to the chain (Techniques).

moonlit
evening
bracelet

You can have the wonderful look of cabochons without stitching a cage for them with these two-hole beauties. This bracelet is simple to stitch, and you'll want to wear it over and over again!

left   right
hole   hole

**WORKING
WITH
TWO-HOLE
CABOCHON
BEADS**
Two-hole
cabochon
beads have a
domed top and
a flat bottom.
Lay the beads
on your bead-
ing mat with
the domed side
facing up. (My
illustrations
show a flat
bead; make
sure the domed
side is always
facing up.) The
instructions will
indicate which
hole to sew or
sew through:
left or right.

make two side strips

1. Thread a needle on 2 yd. (1.8m) of thread, leaving a 4-in. (10cm) tail. Pick up a SuperDuo (bottom hole) and three 11⁰s, and sew up through the same SuperDuo (empty hole). Pick up three 11⁰s, and sew through the same SuperDuo (bottom hole). Retrace the thread path to secure the beads, ending by the tail. Tie a surgeon's knot **(figure 1, blue path)** (Techniques, p. 9).

2. Sew back through a SuperDuo (bottom hole), three 11⁰s, and the SuperDuo (top hole) **(orange path)**.

3. Pick up two 11⁰s, a SuperDuo, and two 11⁰s, and sew back through the SuperDuo (top hole) in the same direction. Retrace the thread path to secure the beads **(red path)**.

4. Sew through two 11⁰s and the SuperDuo (bottom hole) **(green path)**. Pick up three 11⁰s, and sew through the same SuperDuo (empty hole). Pick up three 11⁰s, and sew down through the same SuperDuo (bottom hole) **(pink path)**.

5. Sew through three 11⁰s and a SuperDuo (top hole) **(gray path)**.

6. Repeat steps 3–5 for the desired length of the bracelet, leaving room for the clasp, and end the threads (Techniques). Make a second side strip.

add cabochons

1. Thread a needle on 2 yd. (1.8m) of thread, leaving a 4-in. (10cm) tail. Pick up a side strip. Sew through a SuperDuo (top hole on the end), two 11⁰s, a SuperDuo (bottom hole), and two 11⁰s. Tie a surgeon's knot **(figure 2, orange path)**.

2. Sew through three 11⁰s, a SuperDuo (bottom hole), and two 11⁰s **(blue path)**.

3. Pick up a cabochon bead (right hole), and sew through a middle 11⁰ in the next three-bead group. Repeat until you reach the end of this side strip **(red path)**.

supplies

Bracelet, 8 in. (20cm)

- **25** 6mm two-hole cabochon beads
- 4g SuperDuos
- **65** 3mm crystal bicones
- 2g dragonscale beads
- 5g 11⁰ seed beads
- two-strand box clasp
- Fireline, 6-lb. test
- beading needle, size 11

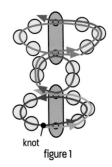

knot
figure 1

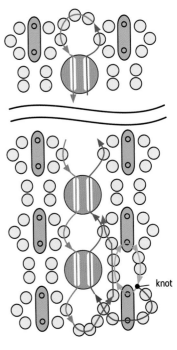

knot

figure 2

4. Pick up three 11ºs, and sew through the middle 11º in an end three-bead group on the second side strip (**green path**).

5. Sew through a cabochon (empty hole) and an 11º (middle bead in the next picot). Repeat to this end of the bracelet (**pink path**).

6. Pick up three 11ºs, and sew through the next six 11ºs on the inside of the first strip (**gray path**).

embellish

1. Pick up three 11ºs, and sew up through the middle 11º in the other side strip (**figure 3, red path**).

2. Sew back through the three 11ºs and up through the middle 11º in the same direction (**orange path**).

3. Sew through a cabochon (right hole) and up through the middle 11º (**pink path**).

4. Repeat steps 1–3.

NOTE: Some dragonscale beads have a different color on each side. Determine which side you would like to display up on the bracelet.

5. Pick up a dragonscale (back to front), an 11º, a crystal, an 11º, and a dragonscale (front to back), and sew up through the middle 11º on the other side strip (**blue path**).

6. Sew back through a dragonscale (back to front), an 11º, a crystal, an 11º, and a dragonscale (front to back), and sew up through the middle 11º in the same direction (**green path**). Retrace the thread path to secure the beads by repeating steps 5 and 6 in this section.

7. Sew through a cabochon (right hole) and up through the middle 11º (**pink path**).

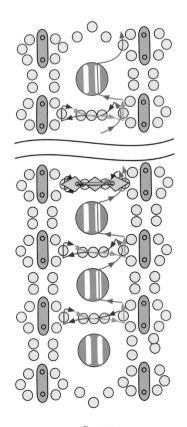

figure 3

8. Repeat steps 5–7 until you have sewn through the third-to-last cabochon and the middle 11º.

9. Repeat steps 1–3 twice (add only three 11ºs at the end, as in the beginning).

add the side picots and clasp

1. Exit the middle 11º, and sew through an 11º, a SuperDuo (top hole), and two 11ºs (**figure 4, gray path**).

2. Pick up an 11º, a crystal, and an 11º, and sew through a middle 11º. Repeat to the end of the bracelet (**blue path**).

3. Sew through an 11º, a SuperDuo (bottom hole or top hole), and an 11º (**pink path**).

4. Pick up two 11ºs and a loop of the clasp (**green path**).

5. Sew through an 11º, pick up an 11º, and sew back through an 11º in the same

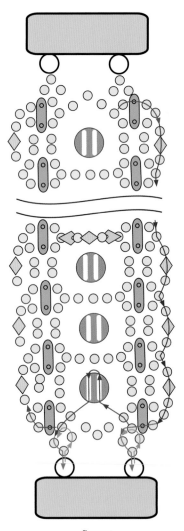

figure 4

direction (**orange path**). Retrace the thread path in steps 4 and 5 to secure the connection.

6. Sew through the next 11º, cabochon (up through the right hole and then down through the left hole), and two 11ºs (**red path**).

7. Repeat steps 4 and 5 to add attach the second loop of the clasp.

8. Exit an 11º, and sew through a SuperDuo (bottom hole) and two 11ºs (**purple path**).

9. Repeat steps 1–7 to complete the other side of the bracelet and add the other half of the clasp. End the threads (Techniques).

sweetheart
necklace

Beautiful colors combine with circle-shaped beads for a magical necklace. Make this piece using RounDuo beads, which are domed on the front and back.

inside   outside
hole   hole

supplies

Necklace, 16 in. (41cm)

- **21** RounDuo beads
- **7** 4mm bicone crystals
- **45** 3mm bicone crystals
- 5g 15º seed beads
- lobster claw clasp
- **2** 5mm jump rings
- 12 in. (30cm) fine cable chain
- 3 in. (7.6cm) chain extender
- Fireline, 4-lb. test
- beading needle, size 11

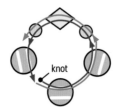

knot

figure 1

figure 2

figure 3

WORKING WITH ROUNDUO BEADS
RounDuo beads are rounded on both sides. Lay the RounDuo beads on your beading mat in a vertical direction. The instructions will indicate which hole to sew through: inside or outside.

start a component

1. Thread a needle on 12 in. (30cm) of thread, leaving a 4-in. (10cm) tail. Pick up two RounDuos (any hole), a 15º seed bead, a 4mm crystal, a 15º, and a RounDuo (any hole), and make a circle by sewing back through all the beads. Tie a surgeon's knot **(figure 1, blue path)** (Techniques, p. 9).

2. Sew back through two RounDuos (inside hole), a 15º, a 4mm, and a 15º **(green path)**.

embellish

1. Pick up three 15ºs, and sew through the next RounDuo (outside hole) **(figure 2, blue path)**.

2. Pick up a 15º, a 3mm crystal, and a 15º, and sew through the next RounDuo (outside hole). Repeat **(green path)**.

3. Pick up three 15ºs, and sew through a 15º, a 4mm, and four 15ºs **(red path)**.

finish the component

1. Pick up five 15ºs, and sew through a 15º, a 3mm, and a 15º **(figure 3, blue path)**.

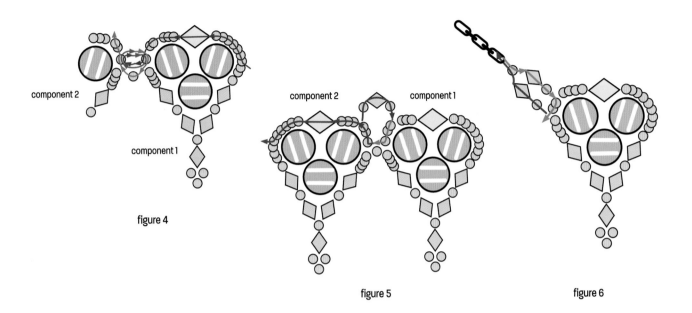

component 2

component 1

figure 4

component 2   component 1

figure 5

figure 6

2. Pick up a 3mm, a 15º, a 3mm, and three 15ºs (**pink path**).

3. Sew back through the 3mm and 15º, and pick up a 3mm (**orange path**).

4. Sew through a 15º, a 3mm, and a 15º. Pick up five 15ºs, and sew through four 15ºs, a 4mm, and four 15ºs (**red path**).

5. Tie a half-hitch knot, and sew through six 15ºs, a 3mm, and a 15º (**green path**). End the threads (Techniques). Repeat the first three sections to make a total of seven components.

connect the components

1. Thread a needle on a new piece of thread about 2 yd. (1.8m) long, leaving an 8-in. (20cm) tail. Pick up a component. On the right side of the component, starting by the 3mm, count four 15ºs. Starting with that fourth 15º, sew up through seven 15ºs, a 4mm, and six 15ºs (**figure 4, blue path**).

2. Pick up a component. On the right

side of the component, starting by the 3mm, count five 15ºs, and sew up through that fifth 15º only (**red path**).

3. Keeping a tight tension, sew down through the 15º you are exiting from in component 1, and sew back up through the same 15º in component 2. Retrace the thread path to secure the connection (**gray path**).

4. Exit a 15º in component 2, sew down through the 15º in component 1, pick up a 15º, and sew through the three 15ºs in component 2 (**green path**).

finish the stitching

1. Exit the fourth 15º from the left of the 4mm in component 2, and pick up a 15º, a 3mm, and a 15º (**figure 5, blue path**).

2. On the left side of component 1, starting by the 4mm, count four 15ºs, and sew down through three 15ºs (**green path**).

3. On the right side of component 2, starting by the 3mm, count five 15ºs, and

sew up through six 15ºs, a 4mm, and six 15ºs (**red path**). Repeat the sections "Connect the Components" (starting at step 2) and "Finish the Stitching" to connect all the components in the same manner.

connect the chain

1. Add a new thread, if necessary (Techniques). Exit the six 15ºs on one end, and pick up a 15º, a 3mm, a 15º, and the chain (**figure 6, blue path**).

2. Sew back through the 15º, pick up a 3mm and a 15º, and sew down through the fifth and sixth 15ºs in the same direction (**green path**). Retrace the thread path to secure the connection, and end the threads. Repeat to connect the chain to the other end of the necklace using the tail from step 4. Cut the chain to the desired length, and add jump rings and desired clasp (Techniques).

spinning pinwheels
bracelet

A Honeycomb bead is shaped just like you would expect: a six-sided honeycomb. This particular two-hole bead is flat on both sides, although a jeweled version would add even more texture.

left
hole

right
hole

WORKING WITH HONEYCOMB BEADS

Honeycomb beads are flat on both sides. Lay the Honeycomb beads on your beading mat in a vertical direction. The instructions will indicate which hole to sew or pass through: left, right, outside, or inside.

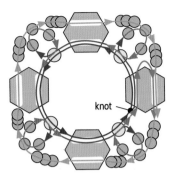

knot

figure 1

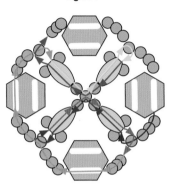

figure 2

supplies

Bracelet, 8 in. (20cm)

- **40** 6mm two-hole Honeycomb beads
- **28** 3mm bicone crystals
- **40** 5x3mm Pinch beads
- 1g 11º seed beads
- 3g 15º seed beads
- two-part clasp
- Fireline, 4-lb. test
- beading needle, size 11

NOTE: Tension control is very important. If the Honeycomb beads start to curl up a lot, your tension is too tight.

make the components

1. Thread a needle on 2 ft. (61cm) of thread, leaving a 4-in. (10cm) tail. Pick up a Honeycomb bead (left hole) and an 11º seed bead a total of four times. Make a circle by sewing back through all the beads (**figure 1, blue path**). Tie a surgeon's knot (Techniques, p. 9).
2. Sew through a Honeycomb (inside hole) and an 11º (**red path**).
3. Pick up three 15º seed beads, and sew back through the 11º in the same direction to make a picot (Techniques) (**pink path**).
4. Repeat steps 2 and 3 around the component.
5. Sew through a Honeycomb (inside

hole), and then sew through the same Honeycomb (outside hole) in the opposite direction (**green path**).
6. Pick up three 15º s, sew through the middle 15º in the picot, pick up three 15º s, and sew through a Honeycomb (outside hole). Repeat this step around the component (**orange path**).

add Pinch beads

NOTE: As you add the Pinch beads, they will raise up and lie in between the Honeycomb beads.

1. Sew through four 15º s (**figure 2, blue path**).
2. Pick up a Pinch bead, three 15º s, and a Pinch, and sew through the adjacent middle 15º (**red path**).
3. Sew back through the Pinch, three 15º s, Pinch, and 15º in the same direction (**pink path**).

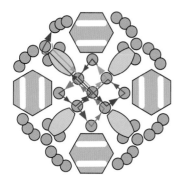

figure 3

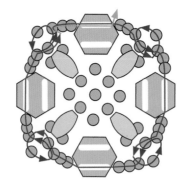

figure 4

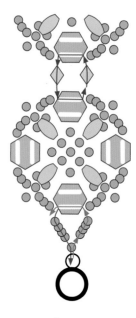

figure 5

4. Sew through three 15ºs, a Honeycomb (outside hole), seven 15ºs, a Honeycomb (outside hole), and four 15ºs (**orange path**).

5. Pick up a Pinch and a 15º, and sew through a middle 15º. Pick up a 15º and a Pinch, and sew through the adjacent middle 15º (**yellow path**).

6. Sew through a Pinch, three 15ºs, a Pinch, and a 15º in the same direction (**gray path**).

add seed beads

1. Sew through a Pinch and three 15ºs (**figure 3, orange path**).

2. Pick up a 15º, and sew through three 15ºs (**gray path**). Pick up a 15º, and sew through three 15ºs (**red path**). Pick up a 15º, and sew through three 15ºs (**pink path**). Pick up a 15º, and sew through three 15ºs, a Pinch, and a 15º in the same direction (**blue path**).

add picots

1. Sew through a 15º, pick up a 15º, and sew down through two 15ºs in the same direction to make a picot (**figure 4, blue path**). Retrace the thread path to reinforce the picot. Sew through three 15ºs, a Honeycomb (outside hole), and four 15ºs (**red path**).

2. Repeat step 1 around the component.

3. Sew through three 15ºs and a Honeycomb (outside hole) (**orange path**). End the tail (Techniques).

4. Leave the working thread to either connect the components or add the clasp. Repeat the first four sections to make other components until you have enough to reach the desired length, minus the clasp.

NOTE: Make sure the components are facing the same way.

connect the components and clasp

1. Exit a Honeycomb (outside hole), pick up a 3mm bicone crystal, a Honeycomb (outside hole of the other component), and a crystal, and sew back through the first Honeycomb (outside hole) in the same direction. Retrace the thread path to reinforce the connection (**figure 5, blue path**).

2. Sew back through a few beads in the component, and end the thread.

3. Repeat steps 1 and 2 to connect the other components.

4. Exit a Honeycomb (outside hole), pick up five 15ºs and half of the clasp (**red path**), and sew back through a 15º. Pick up four 15ºs, and sew back through the first Honeycomb (outside hole) in the same direction (**pink path**). Retrace the thread path to reinforce the thread and secure the clasp. End the thread.

5. Repeat step 4 to add the other clasp half to the other end of the bracelet.

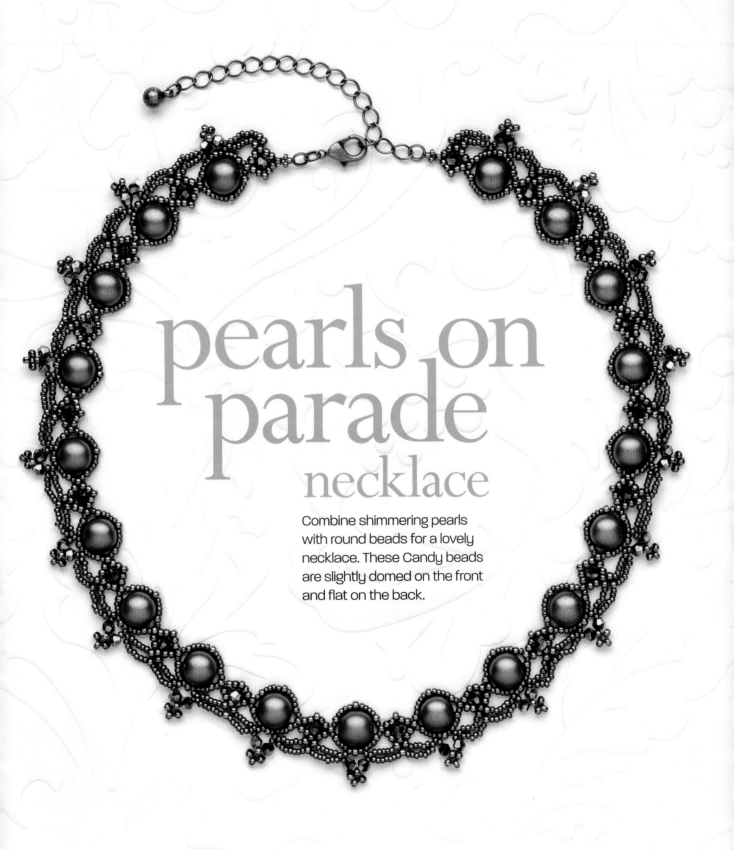

pearls on parade
necklace

Combine shimmering pearls with round beads for a lovely necklace. These Candy beads are slightly domed on the front and flat on the back.

supplies

Necklace, 16 in. (41cm)

- **19** Candy beads
- **59** 3mm bicone crystals
- 8g 11º seed beads
- 8g 15º seed beads
- lobster claw clasp and jump ring
- 3 in. (7.6cm) chain extender
- Fireline, 4-lb. test
- beading needle, size 11

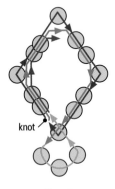

figure 1

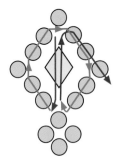

figure 2

begin the necklace

1. Thread a needle on 2 yd. (1.8m) of thread, leaving a 4-in. (10cm) tail. Pick up 12 11ºs, and make a circle by sewing through all the beads again **(figure 1, blue path)**. Tie a surgeon's knot (Techniques, p. 9).

2. Sew through two 11ºs and skip an 11º. Repeat this step twice, then sew through three 11ºs **(green path)**.

3. Pick up three 11ºs, and sew back through the 11º you just exited to make a picot **(orange path)** (Techniques). Retrace the thread path to reinforce the picot.

4. Sew up through two 11ºs only, skip an 11º, and sew up through two 11ºs **(red path)**.

NOTE: The skipped 11ºs will lay on the outside. If they don't, take your needle and pull the beads toward the outside to form a diamond shape.

add crystals

1. Pick up a 3mm bicone crystal **(figure 2, red path)**.

2. Sew up through two 11ºs, skip an 11º, and sew through two 11ºs. Skip an 11º, and sew through two 11ºs. Skip an 11º, and sew through two 11ºs **(green path)**.

3. Sew up through the crystal and down through the next three 11ºs **(blue path)**.

left hole   right hole

WORKING WITH CANDY BEADS
Lay the beads on your beading mat with the slightly domed side facing up in a vertical direction. The instructions will indicate which hole to sew or sew through: right, bottom, top, or empty.

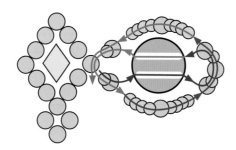

figure 3

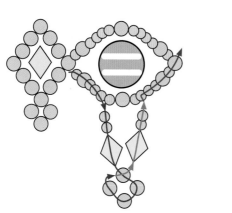

figure 4

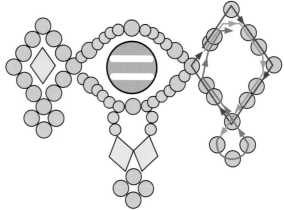

figure 5

add Candy beads

1. Pick up a 15º, an 11º, a Candy bead (right hole), an 11º, a 15º, an 11º, a 15º, and an 11º (**figure 3, blue path**).

2. Sew through the same Candy (empty hole), pick up an 11º and a 15º, and sew down through the 11º in the completed component, a 15º, and an 11º (**green path**).

3. Pick up four 15ºs, an 11º, and four 15ºs, and sew through an 11º, a 15º, an 11º, a 15º, and an 11º (**red path**).

4. Pick up four 15ºs, an 11º, and four 15ºs. Sew through an 11º, a 15º, and an 11º (**pink path**).

continue the necklace

1. Sew through a 15º, an 11º, and three 15ºs. Pick up two 15ºs, a crystal, and four 11ºs (**figure 4, blue path**).

2. Sew back through the first 11º picked up in the same direction, and pull the beads taut. Pick up a crystal and two 15ºs (**green path**).

3. Skip a 15º, an 11º, and a 15º from where you are exiting the component, and sew through three 15ºs, an 11º, a 15º, and an 11º (**red path**).

connect the pieces

1. Pick up eleven 11ºs, and make a circle by sewing back through the 11º you just

exited in the same direction (**figure 5, red path**).

2. Sew through two 11ºs, skip an 11º, sew through two 11ºs, skip an 11º, and sew through three 11ºs (**orange path**).

3. Pick up three 11ºs, and sew back through the 11º you just exited in the same direction to make a picot. Sew back through all the beads to secure the picot, and sew through two 11ºs, skip an 11º, and sew up through two 11ºs (**green path**). Repeat "Add Crystals" to "Connect the Pieces" to the desired length, ending with the component with the crystal in the middle. Don't end the working thread.

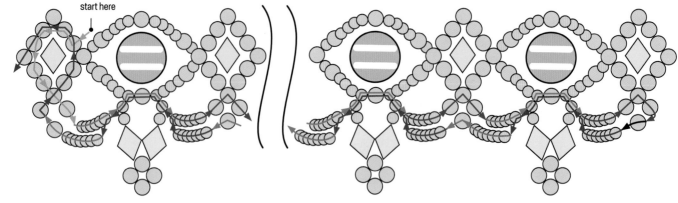

start here

figure 6

add the scallops

1. Thread a needle with 2 yd. (1.8m) of thread, leaving a 4-in. (10cm) tail. Starting on the left side of the necklace, sew up through two 11ºs in the first component, and tie a half-hitch knot (Techniques). Skip an 11º, sew down through two 11ºs, skip an 11º, and sew down through four 11ºs **(figure 6, orange path)**.

2. Pick up six 15ºs, and sew up through two 15ºs in the next component, an 11º, and down through two 15ºs **(green path)**.

3. Pick up six 15ºs, and sew up through three 11ºs in the next component's picot **(red path)**. Repeat steps 2 and 3 to the end of the necklace.

4. Exiting an 11º in the picot, sew through an 11º **(black path)**.

5. Pick up seven 15ºs, and sew up through a 15º in the scallop, two 15ºs in the component, an 11º, two 15ºs in the component, and a 15º in the scallop **(blue path)**.

6 Pick up seven 15ºs, and sew through the middle bottom 11º in the next component **(pink path)**. Repeat steps 5 and 6 to the end of the necklace. Exit the last middle 11º.

7. Sew through four 11ºs, skip an 11º, and sew through two 11ºs. Skip an 11º, and sew through three 11ºs **(gray path)**.

figure 7

add the clasp

1. Using the thread that is exiting the end 11º of the last component, pick up two 15ºs and the jump ring with the attached lobster claw clasp or extender **(figure 7, blue path)**.

2. Sew back through the last 15º just picked up, pick up a 15º, and sew back through the 11º you just exited **(red path)**.

3. Retrace the thread path a few more times to secure the connection, and end the threads (Techniques). Repeat to add a clasp half on the other side of the necklace.

3 square beads

shimmering pyramids
bracelet

It was a pleasure to use Pyramid beads in this bracelet. These beads make a statement, and the pointed tops stand out in the design.

left   right
hole   hole

WORKING WITH PYRAMID (STUD) BEADS
Pyramid beads have a pointed top and a flat bottom. The illustration shows a flat bead. Lay the Pyramids so the pointed side is facing up. The instructions will indicate which hole to sew through: left, right, or empty.

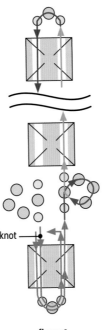

knot

figure 1

supplies
Bracelet, 8 in. (20cm)
- **20** Czech Pyramid beads
- **60** 3mm bicone crystals
- 5g 11º seed beads
- 2g 15º seed beads
- ball-and-socket clasp
- Fireline, 6-lb. test
- beading needle, size 11

NOTE: You will add the Pyramids and make the first picots on the first side of the bracelet. All of the beads will be very wonky until you start attaching the Pyramids and picots to the other side.

begin the bracelet

1. Thread a needle on about 2 yd. (1.8m) of thread, leaving about a 3-in. (7.6cm) tail. Pick up a Pyramid bead (left hole), a 15º seed bead, and an 11º seed bead, and sew back up through the same Pyramid (right hole). Sew back through all the beads, and tie a surgeon's knot **(figure 1, green path)** (Techniques, p. 9).

2. Sew down through a Pyramid (left hole), a 15º, an 11º, a 15º, and the same Pyramid (right hole) **(pink path)**. End the tail (Techniques).

3. Pick up a 15º and four 11ºs **(red path)**.

4. Sew back through the first 11º just picked up in the same direction, and pull the beads taut to make a picot (Techniques). Pick up a 15º and a Pyramid (right hole) **(orange path)**.

5. Repeat steps 3 and 4, ending with an Pyramid, for the desired length of the bracelet, leaving room for the clasp.

6. Pick up a 15º, an 11º, and a 15º, and sew down through the same Pyramid (empty hole) **(blue path)**.

7. Repeat steps 3–6 on the other side of the bracelet. Finish by exiting a Pyramid.

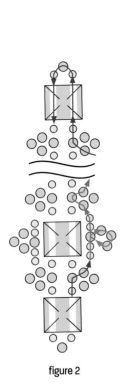

figure 2

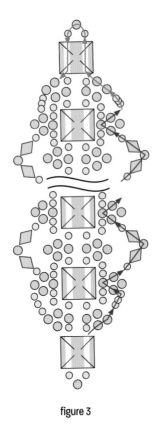

figure 3

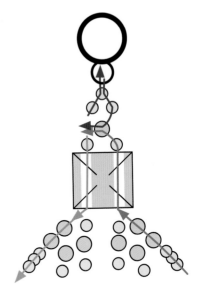

figure 4

embellish

1. Sew through a 15º and two 11ºs in the picot (**figure 2, red path**).

2. Pick up two 15ºs and four 11ºs (**green path**), and sew back through the first 11º in the same direction. Pull the beads taut. Pick up two 15ºs, and sew through three 11ºs in the next picot (**pink path**).

3. Repeat step 2 until you reach the last picot at the end of the bracelet.

4. After picking up the last two 15ºs, sew through two 11ºs, a 15º, a Pyramid (right hole), a 15º, an 11º, a 15º, and a Pyramid (left hole) (**blue path**).

5. Repeat steps 1–4 on the other side of the bracelet. Finish by exiting a Pyramid.

finish the bracelet

1. Sew through two 11ºs in the picot. Pick up three 15ºs, and sew through three 11ºs in the picot (**figure 3, red path**).

2. Pick up a 15º, a 3mm crystal, an 11º, a crystal, and a 15º, and sew through three 11ºs in the picot. Repeat this step until you reach the last picot (**blue path**).

3. Pick up three 15ºs, and sew through two 11ºs in the picot, a Pyramid (right hole), a 15º, an 11º, a 15º, and a Pyramid (left hole) (**green path**).

4. Repeat steps 1–3 to complete the other side of the bracelet. Then, retrace the thread path, EXCEPT skip the 11º in step 2 and sew through the next crystal. This will make the 11º protrude. If this bead is not protruding, pull it out with the needle. Continue to the end of the bracelet.

add the clasp

1. Sew through the beadwork to exit an end 11º (**figure 4, green path**).

2. Pick up two 15ºs and the clasp (**red path**).

3. Sew back through the 15º, pick up a 15º, and sew back through the 11º in the same direction (**blue path**). Retrace the thread path to secure the clasp.

4. Sew through a 15º, a Pyramid (left hole), two 11ºs, and three 15ºs (**orange path**).

5. Repeat step 1–4 on the other end of the bracelet. End the thread (Techniques).

lacy silk
bracelet

This slinky bracelet shows off Silky beads to perfection. These sleek beads are shaped like diamonds, and most have a front side that displays a grooved surface. Some Silky beads are flat on both sides, which makes for a very smooth look and feel, indeed!

supplies

Bracelet, 8 in. (20cm)
- **20** Silky beads
- 5g 15º seed beads
- ball-and-socket clasp
- Fireline, 4-lb. test
- beading needle, size 11

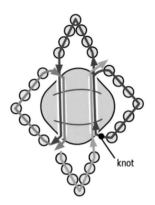

figure 1

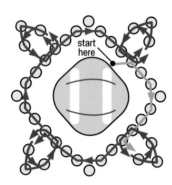

figure 2

left hole   right hole

WORKING WITH SILKY BEADS
Some Silky beads have a bottom and top side, and some have two flat surfaces. The Silkys I used have a top with a grooved surface and a flat bottom. Place the beads on your mat with the grooved surface facing up and the holes running vertically. The instructions will indicate which hole to sew through: left or right.

make the first component

NOTE: Keep a tight tension as you work.

1. Thread a needle on a comfortable length of thread, leaving a 4-in. (10cm) tail. Pick up a Silky bead (right hole) and seven 15º seed beads, and connect the beads into a circle by passing back through all the beads in the same direction. Tie a surgeon's knot, and sew through the Silky (right hole) (Techniques, p. 9) **(figure 1, blue path)**.

2. Pick up seven 15ºs, and sew through the Silky (left hole) **(red path)**.

3. Pick up seven 15ºs, and sew back through the Silky (left hole) in the same direction **(green path)**.

4. Pick up seven 15ºs, and sew through the Silky (right hole) **(orange path)**.

make the picots

1. Sew through three 15ºs to the right of the Silky, skip a 15º, and sew through four 15ºs **(figure 2, orange path)**.

2. Pick up three 15ºs, and sew back through the last two 15ºs in the base in the same direction to make a picot (Techniques). Sew through the first 15º, skip a 15º, and sew through the last 15º in the picot and the two 15ºs in the base **(blue path)**.

3. Sew through two 15ºs, skip a 15º, and sew through four 15ºs **(red path)**.

4. Repeat steps 2 and 3 around the component, ending with step 2.

make the remaining components

1. Keep a tight tension. Make sure the Silkys are facing the same direction. After completing the fourth picot, sew through three 15ºs **(figure 3, green path)**.

2. Pick up three 15ºs and a Silky (right hole) **(orange path)**. Pick up seven 15ºs, and make a circle by sewing back through the Silky (right hole) **(blue path)**. Pick up seven 15ºs, and sew through the Silky (left hole) **(red path)**. Pick up seven 15ºs, and make a circle by sewing back through the Silky (left hole) **(gray path)**.

3. Pick up three 15ºs, and sew through the middle 15º of the previous component and six 15ºs, skip a 15º, sew through six 15ºs, skip a 15º, and sew through four 15ºs in the component you just created **(pink path)**. Repeat "Make the Picots" (starting at step 2) and "Make the Remaining Components" until you have reached the desired length, ending with "Make the Picots." Be sure to leave room for the clasp.

add the clasp and connect the picots

1. Sew through the beadwork to exit an end 15º. Pick up two 15ºs and half of the clasp **(red path)**.

2. Sew back through the 15º, pick up a 15º, and sew back through the 15º you first exited in the same direction **(green path)**. Retrace the thread path to reinforce the clasp.

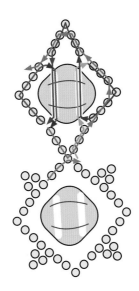

figure 3

3. Sew through six 15ºs, skip a 15º, and sew through two 15ºs (in the base), two 15ºs (in the picot), and a 15º (the middle bead of the next picot) **(gray path)**.

4. Pick up a 15º, and sew down through the middle 15º of the picot and up through the middle 15º of the next picot. Repeat to secure the picot you just created **(orange path)**.

5. Sew through a 15º in the picot and two 15ºs in the base, skip a 15º, sew through two 15ºs in the base, two 15ºs in the picot, and up through the middle 15º of the next picot **(blue path)**.

6. Repeat steps 4 and 5 until you have completed the last picot on this side of the bracelet.

7. Sew through a 15º in the picot and two 15ºs in the base. Skip a 15º, and sew through seven 15ºs in the base **(pink path)**.

8. Repeat steps 1–7 to attach the remaining clasp and embellish the other side of the bracelet. End the threads (Techniques).

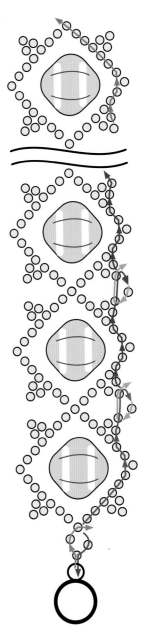

figure 4

stained glass
earrings

QuadraTile beads form the center of this sparkling, light-filled design. Shiny SuperDuos and a dusting of seed beads complete these lively earrings.

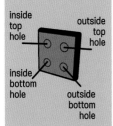

inside top hole | outside top hole
inside bottom hole | outside bottom hole

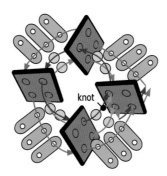

knot

figure 1

make the component bottom

1. Thread a needle on about 1 yd. (.9m) of thread, leaving a 3-in. (7.6cm) tail. Pick up a QuadtraTile (inside top hole) and a 15º a total of four times. Sew back through all the beads one more time. Tie a surgeon's knot **(figure 1, blue path)** (Techniques, p. 9).

2. At the knot, sew through a QuadraTile (inside top hole), and then sew through the same QuadraTile (inside bottom hole) **(orange path)**.

3. Pick up a 15º, and sew through the next QuadraTile (inside bottom hole). Repeat around the component **(green path)**.

4. After exiting the last QuadraTile, sew through the outside bottom hole of the same QuadraTile **(red path)**.

5. Pick up three SuperDuos, and sew through the next QuadraTile (outside bottom hole). Repeat around the component **(pink path)**.

embellish

1. Sew through the next three Super-Duos (used holes), and sew up through the last SuperDuo (empty hole) **(figure 2, orange path)**.

2. Pick up four 15ºs **(green path)**.

3. Sew back through the first 15º picked up in the same direction and the next

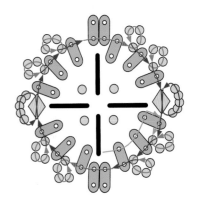

figure 2

SuperDuo (empty hole). Pull taut to make a picot (Techniques) **(red path)**.

4. Repeat steps 2 and 3.

5. Pick up two SuperDuos; sew through the empty hole of the next SuperDuo **(pink path)**.

6. Repeat steps 2–4.

7. Pick up a 3mm crystal and five 15ºs, and make a circle by sewing back through crystal in the same direction you are exiting and continuing through the next SuperDuo (empty hole). Pull the beads taut **(blue path)**.

8. Repeat steps 2–7 one more time around the component.

make the picots

NOTE: Make sure you are working on the front of the earring.

1. Retrace the thread path through the next two picots (**figure 3, green and red paths**) to secure the picots.

2. Exit the SuperDuo, pick up a 15º, and sew up through the next SuperDuo (empty hole). Pick up a crystal, and sew through the next SuperDuo (empty hole). Pick up a 15º, and sew through next SuperDuo (top hole) (**pink path**).

3. Retrace the thread path through the next two picots (**green and red paths**). Then sew through two 15ºs, skip a 15º, and sew through two 15ºs and a Super-Duo (**blue path**). Retrace the thread path through the next two picots (**green and red paths**).

4. Repeat steps 2 and 3, and then retrace the thread path through the next two picots one more time (**green and red paths**).

finish the earrings

1. Sew through the beadwork to exit the bottom crystal (**figure 4, red path**).

2. Pick up four 15ºs, a crystal, and three 15ºs, and sew back through the crystal and 15º. Pick up three 15ºs, and sew back through the crystal in the same direction. Retrace the thread path to secure the connection (**green path**).

3. Sew through the beadwork to exit the crystal on the opposite side of the path (**orange path**).

4. Pick up eight 15ºs, an earring finding, and four 15ºs (**pink path**).

figure 3

5. Make a circle by sewing back through the fourth 15º from the very first bead picked up. Pick up three 15ºs, and sew through the crystal in the same direction (**blue path**). Retrace the thread path to secure the earring finding.

6. Sew through a SuperDuo, a 15º, and a SuperDuo, and continue down through the other hole of the same SuperDuo and a QuadraTile (outside bottom hole) (**gray path**).

7. Sew up through the QuadraTile (outside top hole) on the same side you are exiting (you will be going the opposite direction as you exit the hole) (**teal path**).

8. Pick up a 15º, a crystal, and a 15º, and sew through the next QuadraTile (outside top hole). Repeat around the component (**purple path**). Retrace the thread path to secure the beads, and end the threads (Techniques).

9. Repeat to make a second earring.

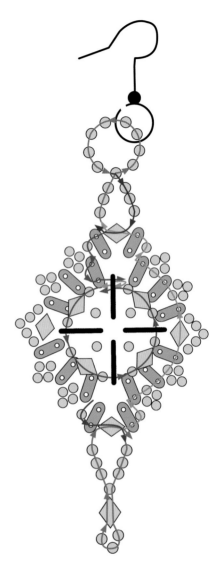

figure 4

enlaced tile
bracelet

Tile beads are small, square shaped beads that are incredibly versatile. You can use any combination of brilliant colors in this striking design.

supplies

Bracelet, 8 in. (20cm)

- **15** Tile beads
- **48** 3mm bicone crystals
- 2g SuperDuos
- 4g O-Beads
- 5g 11º seed beads
- 2g 15º seed beads
- ball-and-socket clasp
- Fireline, 6-lb. test
- beading needle, size 11

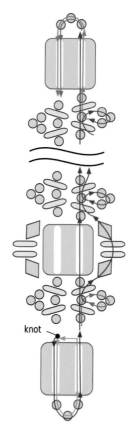

knot

figure 1

make the bracelet

1. Thread a needle on a comfortable length of thread, leaving a 4-in. (10cm) tail. Pick up a Tile bead (left hole) by passing down through the bead, pick up three 11º seed beads, and then sew up through the Tile (right hole). Sew back through the beads, and tie a surgeon's knot (Techniques, p. 9) **(figure 1, orange path)**.

2. After tying the knot, sew down through a Tile (left hole), three 11ºs, and a Tile (right hole) **(purple path)**.

3. Pick up an 11º, an O-Bead, an 11º, an O-Bead, an 11º, and a Tile (right hole). Repeat this step for the desired length of the bracelet, leaving room for the clasp **(blue path)**.

4. Pick up three 11ºs, and sew down through the Tile (left hole). Snug the beads together, but not too tight **(brown path)**.

5. Repeat step 3, adding 11ºs and O-Beads between the existing Tiles. Sew through the beadwork to exit the next Tile (right hole).

6. Sew through an 11º, an O-Bead, and an 11º. Pick up three 11ºs **(pink path)**.

7. Sew back through the 11º you originally exited (in the same direction) and continue through an O-Bead. Pick up a 3mm crystal, two O-Beads, and a crystal **(gray path)**.

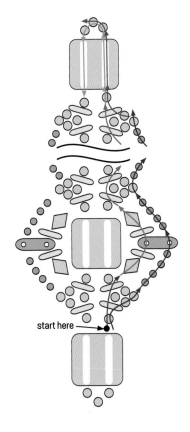

figure 2

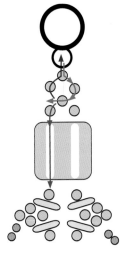

figure 3

8. Skip an 11º, sew through an O-Bead and an 11º, and pick up three 11ºs (**red path**).

9. Repeat steps 7 and 8 until you have picked up the last three 11ºs to make the last picot; then, sew back through the 11º in the same direction and continue through an O-Bead, an 11º, a Tila (right hole), three 11ºs, and a Tila (left hole) (**green path**).

10. Repeat steps 6–9 to complete the other side of the bracelet, exiting the last Tile.

embellish the bracelet

1. Sew through an 11º and two O-Beads (**figure 2, red path**).

2. Sew through a crystal and an O-Bead, pick up a SuperDuo, and sew through an O-Bead and a crystal (**green path**). Sew through two O-Beads (**pink path**). Repeat to the end of the bracelet, exiting the last O-Bead.

3. Sew through an 11º, a Tile (right hole), three 11ºs, and a Tile (left hole) (**orange path**).

4. Repeat steps 1–3 to complete the other side of the bracelet.

5. Exit a Tile (right hole), and sew through an 11º, an O-Bead and two 11ºs (**gray path**).

6. Pick up four 15ºs, sew through a SuperDuo (empty hole), pick up four 15ºs, and sew through an 11º. Repeat this step to the end of the bracelet (**blue path**).

7. Sew through an 11º, an O-Bead, an 11º, a Tila (right side), and two 11ºs (**purple path**).

add the clasp

1. Pick up two 11ºs and the clasp (**figure 3, blue path**).

2. Sew back through the 11º, pick up an 11º, and sew back through the 11º you exited in the same direction (**green path**). Retrace the thread path to secure the connection.

3. Sew through an 11º and a Tila (left side) (**purple path**).

4. Repeat steps 5–7 of "Embellish the Bracelet," and then continue to "Add the Clasp" to complete the other end of the bracelet. End the threads (Techniques).

tea leaf
bracelet

I love the look of a simple square. A Tila bead is a nice, small square shape, and it can be used in many different ways. Try this pattern with Tile beads as well! They will be slightly thicker, but the look will be very similar.

left
hole

right
hole

**WORKING
WITH TILA
BEADS**

Tila beads have
two different
sides: one
side is flat and
the other has
a very slight
curve. Place the
curved side up.
The instructions
will indicate
which hole to
sew through:
left or right.

supplies
Bracelet, 8 in. (20cm)

- 2g Tila beads
- **52** 3mm bicone crystals
- 4g SuperDuos
- 5g 15º seed beads
- ball-and-socket clasp
- Fireline, 6-lb. test
- beading needle, size 11

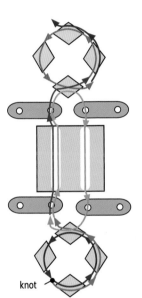

knot

figure 1

make the length

1. Thread a needle on about 2 yd. (1.8m)
of thread, leaving a 4-in. (10cm) tail.
Pick up four 3mm crystals, and make
a circle by sewing back through all the
beads. Tie a surgeon's knot **(figure 1,
blue path)** (Techniques, p. 9).

2. At the knot, sew through three
crystals **(green path)**. End the tail.

3. Pick up a SuperDuo, a Tila (left hole),
a SuperDuo, a crystal, and a SuperDuo;
sew down through the same Tila (right
hole), pick up a SuperDuo, and sew
through the next crystal **(orange path)**.

4. Sew through the next SuperDuo, Tila
(left hole), SuperDuo, and crystal
(red path).

5. Pick up three crystals, and sew back
through the first crystal you exited in
the same direction. Retrace the thread
path to tighten the circle **(pink path)**.

6. Sew through two crystals **(gray path)**.

7. Repeat steps 3–6 to the desired length,
leaving room for the clasp.

embellish the bracelet

1. Exit the end crystal, sew through a crystal and a SuperDuo (empty hole), pick up three 15⁰s, and sew through a Tila (right hole) (**figure 2, blue path**).

2. Pick up three 15⁰s and sew through a SuperDuo (empty hole), a crystal, and a SuperDuo (empty hole). Pick up three 15⁰s and sew through a Tila (right hole) (**gray path**). Repeat this step until you have passed through the last Tila.

3. Pick up three 15⁰s, and sew through a SuperDuo (empty hole) (**yellow path**) and two crystals (**green path**).

4. Repeat steps 1–3 to complete the other side of the bracelet.

5. Exiting the end crystal, sew through a crystal, a SuperDuo (inside hole) and a 15⁰ (by the SuperDuo inside hole) (**orange path**).

6. Pick up three 15⁰s, skip the Tila, sew through a 15⁰ (by the SuperDuo inside hole), a SuperDuo (inside hole), a crystal, a SuperDuo (inside hole), and a 15⁰ (by the SuperDuo inside hole) (**red path**). Repeat this step until you have to pick up the last three 15⁰s.

7. Pick up three 15⁰s, and sew through a 15⁰ (by the SuperDuo inside hole), a SuperDuo (inside hole), and three crystals (**pink path**).

8. Repeat steps 5–7 to complete the other side of the bracelet.

NOTE: The skipped 15⁰ may lay under the thread. Take the needle and pull that skipped 15⁰ out toward the outside of the bracelet.

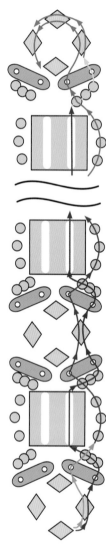

figure 2

add the clasp

1. Exit a crystal, sew through a SuperDuo (inside hole) and two 15⁰s, skip a 15⁰, and sew through two 15⁰s, a SuperDuo (inside hole), and a crystal. Repeat along the bracelet (**figure 3, red path**)

2. Sew through the end crystal (**green path**). Pick up two 15⁰s and the clasp (**orange path**).

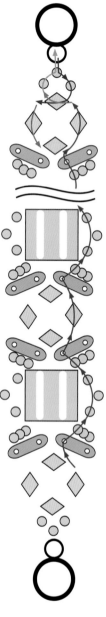

figure 3

3. Sew back through the last 15⁰, pick up a 15⁰, and sew back through a crystal in the same direction (**blue path**). Retrace the thread path to secure the clasp.

4. Sew through a crystal (**pink path**).

5. Repeat steps 1–4 on the other side of the bracelet to add the other half of the clasp. End the threads (Techniques).

4 triangular beads

arrow
bracelet

Create a bracelet inspired by geometry with Kheops beads. These triangular beads can be tricky to use, as they have two holes that run through the bottom of the triangle and exit on both sides of one corner.

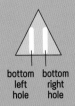

bottom
left
hole

bottom
right
hole

WORKING WITH KHEOPS BEADS

Kheops beads are triangular and flat on both sides. Place the beads on your mat with the holes in a vertical direction. The instructions will indicate which hole to sew through: left, bottom to side; left, side to bottom; right, bottom to side; or right, side to bottom.

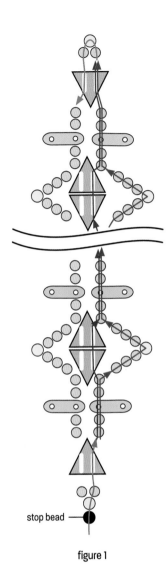

stop bead

figure 1

begin the bracelet

NOTE: You will add the Kheops and the SuperDuos on the first side of the bracelet, but all of the beads will be very wonky until you start attaching beads to the other side.

1. Thread a needle on a comfortable length of thread. Pick up a stop bead, an 11º seed bead, a 15º seed bead, and a Kheops bead (right hole, bottom to side hole) (Techniques, p. 9) **(figure 1, pink path).**

2. Pick up two 15ºs, a SuperDuo, two 15ºs, a Kheops (right hole, side to bot-

supplies

Bracelet, 8 in. (20cm)

- 5g Kheops beads
- 3g SuperDuos
- 1g 11º seed beads
- 2.5g 15º seed beads
- ball-and-socket clasp
- stop bead
- Fireline, 6-lb. test
- beading needle, size 12

tom), and a Kheops (right hole, bottom to side). Repeat until you reach the desired length, ending with a Kheops (right hole, side to bottom), leaving room for the clasp **(blue path)**.

3. Pick up a 15º, an 11º, and a 15º, and sew through the same Kheops (left hole, bottom to side) you are currently exiting **(green path)**.

4. Repeat steps 1–3, sewing through the existing Kheops beads and adding the other beads as instructed. After exiting the last Kheops, pick up a 15º and sew through the next 11º, 15º, and Kheops (right hole, bottom to side). Remove the stop bead.

5. Sew through two 15ºs, a SuperDuo, and two 15ºs. Pick up three 15ºs, an 11º, and three 15ºs, and sew through two 15ºs, a SuperDuo, and two 15ºs. Repeat this step to the end of this side, then sew through a Kheops (right hole, side to bottom) **(red path)**.

6. Sew through a 15º, an 11º, a 15º, and a Kheops (left hole, bottom to side) **(green path)**.

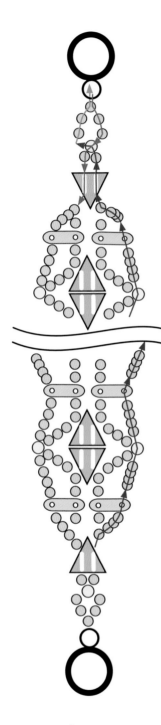

figure 2

7. Repeat steps 5 and 6 on the other side of the bracelet. Exit an end Kheops.

finish the bracelet

1. Sew through a 15º, pick up three 15ºs, and sew through a SuperDuo (empty hole).

2. Pick up four 15ºs, and sew through an 11º. Pick up four 15ºs, and sew through a SuperDuo (empty hole). Repeat to the end of the bracelet **(figure 2, red path)**.

3. Pick up three 15ºs, and sew through a 15º, a Kheops (right hole, side to bottom), a 15º, and an 11º **(blue path)**.

4. Pick up three 15ºs and half of the clasp **(green path)**.

5. Sew back through the last 15º, pick up two 15ºs, and sew through the 11º (in the same direction), the next 15º, and the Kheops (left hole, bottom to side) **(pink path)**.

6. Repeat steps 1–5 to complete the other half of the bracelet. End the threads (Techniques).

sweet
floweret
pendant

Transform beautiful Trinity beads, which have three round shapes fused together in a triangular formation, into a romantic pendant. You will enjoy this delicate design!

supplies

- 2g Trinity beads
- **58** 3mm bicone crystals
- 3g SuperDuos
- 1g 11º seed beads
- 2g 15º seed beads
- 18x13mm oval cabochon (mine is Lunasoft)
- finished neck chain
- Fireline, 4-lb. test
- beading needle, size 11

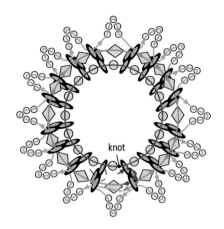

figure 1

top holes

base hole

WORKING WITH TRINITY BEADS

Trinity beads have three holes. Place the beads on your mat with two holes as the top and one hole as the base. The instructions will indicate which hole to sew through: top or bottom.

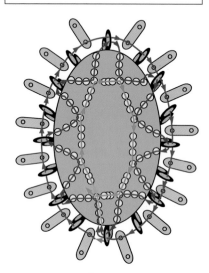

figure 2

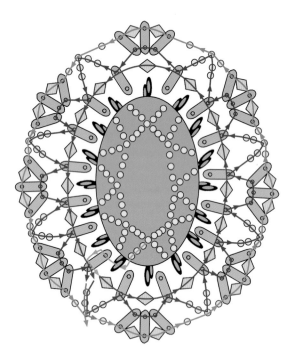

figure 3

make the pendant front

NOTE: The oval takes shape when the cabochon is placed in the beadwork.

1. Thread a needle on 1 yd. (.9m) of thread, leaving a 4-in. (10cm) tail. Pick up a repeating pattern of a Trinity bead (it doesn't matter which hole you start with—this will be considered one of the top holes for the front of the pendant) and an 11º seed bead a total of 16 times. Make a circle by sewing back through all of the beads. Tie a surgeon's knot (Techniques, p. 9) **(figure 1, red path)**.

2. Sew through the next Trinity, and continue through the next empty hole of the same Trinity (this will determine the other top hole of the crystal for the front of the pendant) **(blue path)**.

3. Pick up a 3mm crystal, and sew through the corresponding hole of the next Trinity (top hole). Repeat around the circle **(green path)**.

4. Pick up five 15ºs, skip the next crystal, and sew through the next

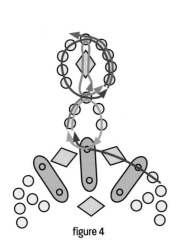

figure 4

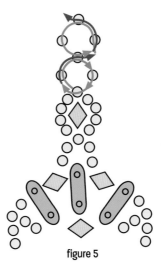

figure 5

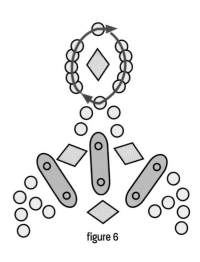

figure 6

Trinity (top hole). Repeat around the circle and exit a Trinity (top hole) (**orange path**).

make the pendant back

1. Flip the pendant over to work on the back side. Exiting the Trinity (top hole), sew through the empty hole of the same Trinity (now called the "bottom" hole) (**figure 2, pink path**).

2. Pick up a SuperDuo, and sew through the next Trinity (bottom hole). Repeat around the circle (**blue path**).

3. Pick up seven 15ºs, skip a Trinity, and sew through the next Trinity (bottom hole). Repeat around the circle (**red path**).

4. Sew through the next four 15ºs (**orange path**).

5. Insert the cabochon, front side down, underneath the 15ºs just added. The 15ºs will lie on top of the backside of the cabochon.

6. Pick up three 15ºs, and sew through the middle 15º of the next group of seven 15ºs. Repeat around the pendant (**green path**). Retrace the thread path to secure the cabochon in place.

continue

1. Exit a middle 15º, sew through three 15ºs, a Trinity (bottom hole), and a SuperDuo, and sew up through the

empty hole of the same SuperDuo (**figure 3, orange path**).

2. Pick up a 3mm crystal, and sew through the next SuperDuo (empty hole). Repeat around the pendant (**blue path**).

3. Pick up five 15ºs, and sew through the next SuperDuo. Pick up three SuperDuos, and sew through the next SuperDuo. Repeat around the pendant (**red path**).

4. Sew through the next three 15ºs (**pink path**).

5. Pick up a 15º, sew through a SuperDuo (empty hole), pick up a crystal, sew through SuperDuo (empty hole), pick up a crystal, sew through a SuperDuo (empty hole), pick up a 15º, and sew through the next middle 15º in the group of five. Repeat around the pendant (**green path**).

make the bail

1. Flip the pendant over and work on the front. Sew through the beadwork to exit a SuperDuo between the crystals (**figure 4, blue path**).

2. Pick up five 15ºs, and sew back through the SuperDuo in the same direction. Retrace the thread path to reinforce the stitch (**orange path**).

3. Sew through three 15ºs (**pink path**). Pick up a crystal and a 15º, and sew back

through the crystal and 15º in the same direction (**green path**).

4. Pick up four 15ºs, sew through a 15º, pick up four 15ºs, and sew back through a 15º in the same direction (**red path**). Sew back through five 15ºs (**gray path**).

complete the bail

1. Pick up three 15ºs, and sew back through the 15º you are currently exiting in the same direction. Retrace the thread path to tighten the beads (**figure 5, green path**).

2. Sew through two 15ºs (**blue path**).

3. Repeat step 1 and 2 in the opposite direction.

finish the pendant

1. Flip the pendant over so you are working on the back. Fold the bail in half. Exit a 15º on the end, pick up five 15ºs, and sew through the 15º below the crystal in the same direction. You are creating a circle of beads behind the crystal (**figure 6, red path**).

2. Exit a 15º below the crystal, pick up five 15ºs, and sew back through the 15º you originally exited in step 1 (**red path**) in the same direction (**blue path**). Retrace the thread path to reinforce the connection, and end the threads (Techniques).

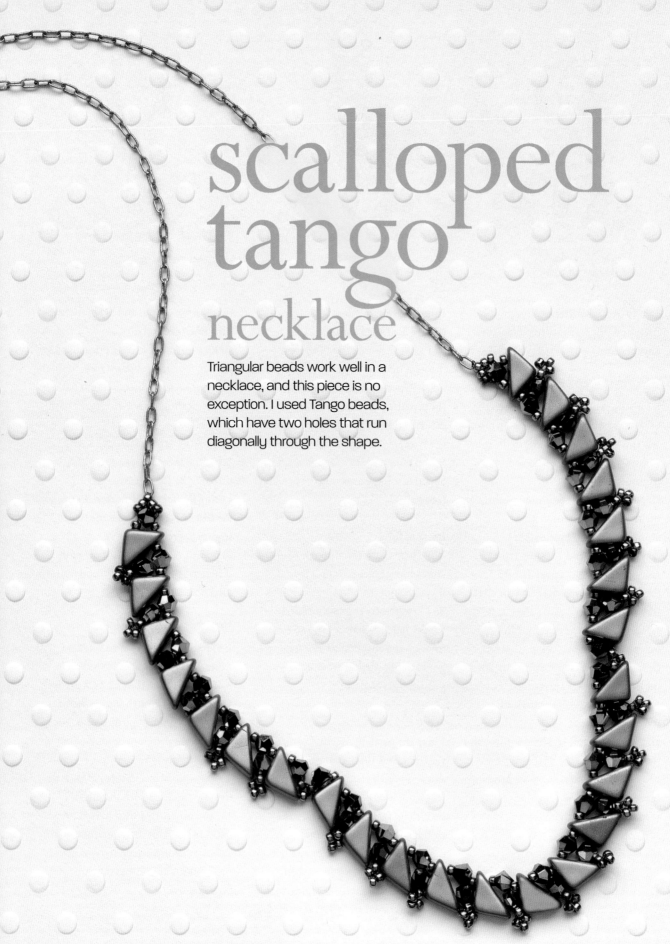

scalloped tango

necklace

Triangular beads work well in a necklace, and this piece is no exception. I used Tango beads, which have two holes that run diagonally through the shape.

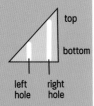

top

bottom

left hole   right hole

WORKING WITH TANGO BEADS

Tango beads are triangular shaped and flat on both sides. Place the beads on your mat with the holes in a vertical direction. The instructions will indicate which hole to sew through: left or right.

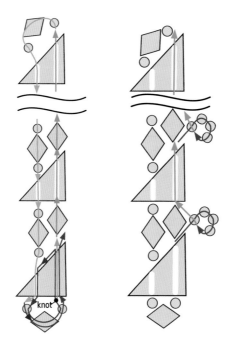

figure 1   figure 2

knot

supplies

Necklace, 16 in. (41cm)

- 5g Tango beads
- **50** 3mm bicone crystals
- 3g 15º seed beads
- 10 in. (25cm) cable chain
- **2** 5mm jump rings
- lobster claw clasp
- chain extender
- Fireline, 6-lb. test
- beading needle, size 12

make the components

1. Thread a needle on 1½ yd. (1.4m) thread, leaving a 4-in. (10cm) tail. Pick up a Tango bead (right hole, bottom to top), sew down through the empty hole of the same Tango (left hole), and pick up a 15º seed bead, a 3mm crystal, and a 15º. Retrace the thread path, and tie a surgeon's knot (Techniques, p. 9) **(figure 1, blue path)**.

2. Exit by the knot, and sew through the Tango (right hole) **(orange path)**.

3. Pick up a repeating pattern of a crystal and a Tango (right hole, bottom to top) seven times **(green path)**.

4. Pick up a 15º, a crystal, and a 15º, and sew through the empty hole of the same Tango. Pick up a 15º, a crystal, and a 15º, and sew through the empty hole of the next Tango. Repeat this step to the end of the bracelet **(pink path)**.

5. Sew through a 15º, a crystal, a 15º, and a Tango (right hole) **(red path)**.

NOTE: The component will have a curve to it.

add the picots

NOTE: Only one side of the component will have picots.

1. Pick up four 15ºs **(figure 2, red path)**. Sew back through the first 15º in the same direction to make a picot (Techniques), and continue through the next Tango (right side) **(green path)**.

2. Repeat step 1 to the end of the component. End the tail (Techniques), but leave the working thread; you will use it to connect the components later.

3. Repeat "Make the Components" and "Add the Picots" for a total of three components: Make two components with seven Tangos and one component with 11 Tangos.

seven-Tango component   eleven-Tango component

figure 3

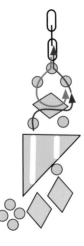

figure 4

connect the components

NOTE: Before you add a component, make sure all the Tangos in all three components are facing the same way.

1. Begin with a seven-Tango component working thread: Sew through a 15º at the end of the component, and then sew down through a 15º at the corresponding end of the 11-Tango component. Pick up a 15º (**figure 3, blue path**). Sew through all three 15ºs a few times to secure the connection (**orange path**). End the working thread.

2. Repeat on the other end to connect the other seven-Tango component.

connect the chain

1. Add a new thread to one end of a side component, and sew through the beadwork to exit an end crystal (**figure 4, blue path**).

2. Pick up two 15ºs and the end of the chain (**red path**).

3. Sew back through the 15º, pick up a 15º, and sew back through the crystal in the same direction (**green path**). Retrace the thread path to secure the connection. End the thread.

4. Repeat steps 1–3 on the other end of the necklace.

5. Connect a jump ring and the chain extender to one end of the necklace. Connect a jump ring and lobster claw clasp to the other end (Techniques).

princess ava
earrings

Create a cute pair of earrings with AVA beads. This set will make you feel like royalty!

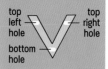
supplies

- **2** AVA beads
- **12** 3mm bicone crystals
- **14** SuperDuos
- 1g 15º seed beads
- **2** 12x6mm Thunder Polish teardrops
- pair of earring findings
- Fireline, 6-lb. test
- beading needle, size 11

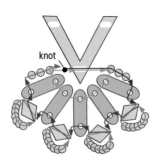

knot

figure 1

begin the earrings

1. Thread a needle on 1 yd. (.9m) of thread, leaving a 4-in. (10cm) tail. Pick up an AVA bead (bottom hole, left to right), a 15º seed bead, five SuperDuos, and a 15º, and sew back through the AVA (bottom hole) in the same direction. Sew through the beads one more time, ending by the tail. Tie a surgeon's knot (Techniques, p. 9) **(figure 1, orange path).**

2. Sew back through the AVA (bottom hole) and a 15º, pick up two 15ºs, and sew through the next SuperDuo (empty hole) **(blue path).**

3. Pick up a 3mm crystal and seven 15ºs **(green path).**

4. Sew back through the crystal in the same direction and continue through the next SuperDuo (empty hole). Make sure the bead are snug **(red path).**

5. Repeat steps 3 and 4 three more times.

6. Pick up two 15ºs, and sew through a 15º **(pink path).**

7. Sew back through the AVA (bottom hole), three 15ºs, and the SuperDuo **(blue path).**

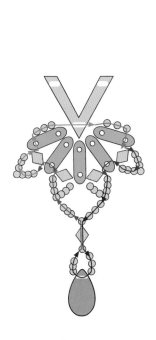

figure 2

figure 3

continue making the earrings

1. Sew through three 15ºs, skip a 15º, and sew through three 15ºs and the next SuperDuo (**figure 2, red path**).

2. Sew through four 15ºs, pick up four 15ºs, a crystal, four 15ºs, a teardrop, and three 15ºs (**blue path**).

3. Sew back through the 15º before the crystal, the crystal, and the 15º after the crystal in the same direction. Pick up three 15ºs, and sew through four 15ºs (in the next picot) and a SuperDuo (**pink path**).

4. Sew through three 15ºs, skip a 15º, and sew through three 15ºs, a SuperDuo, three 15ºs, and the AVA (bottom hole) (**orange path**).

Finish the earrings

1. Sew through two 15ºs, pick up four 15ºs, and sew through the AVA (top right hole). Pick up a 15º, two SuperDuos, and a 15º, and sew through the AVA (top left hole). Pick up four 15ºs, and sew through two 15ºs and the AVA (bottom hole) (**figure 3, blue path**).

2. Sew through six 15ºs, the AVA (top right hole), and a 15º, pick up two 15ºs, and sew up through the next SuperDuo (empty hole). Pick up a crystal, and sew through the next SuperDuo (empty hole). Pick up two 15ºs, and sew through a 15º and two SuperDuos (**red path**).

3. Sew through three 15ºs, a SuperDuo, and a crystal (**green path**).

4. Pick up four 15ºs, a crystal, five 15ºs, an earring finding, and four 15ºs, and sew back through the 15º above the crystal, the crystal, and the 15º below the crystal in the same direction. Pick up three 15ºs, and sew through the next crystal in the same direction (**orange path**). Retrace the thread path to secure the connection, and end the threads (Techniques).

5. Repeat to make another earring.

snow crystal pendant

A delicate, triangle-shaped bead offers numerous possibilities for jewelry design. This glittering pendant is just one beautiful way to display the beads.

left   right
hole   hole

**WORKING
WITH
TRIANGLE
BEADS**
Lay the beads
out on the
beading mat
all facing
the same
direction. The
instructions
will indicate
which hole to
sew through:
front to back
(right or left) or
back to front
(right or left).

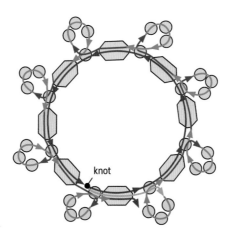

figure 1

supplies

- **8** Triangle beads
- **10** 4mm fire-polished
  round beads
- 4g SuperDuos
- 3g 11º seed beads
- 2g 15º seed beads
- 12mm rivoli
- finished neck chain
- Fireline, 6-lb. test
- beading needle, size 11

begin the pendant

1. Thread a needle on 2 yd. (1.8m) of
thread, leaving a 4-in. (10cm) tail. Pick
up a repeating pattern of an 11º seed
bead and a fire-polished round bead a
total of eight times, and make a circle
by sewing back through all the beads.
Tie a surgeon's knot (Techniques, p. 9)
(figure 1, blue path).
2. At the knot, sew through an 11º, a
round, and an 11º **(orange path)**.
3. Pick up three 11ºs, and sew back
through the 11º you originally exited
in the same direction to create a picot
(Techniques) **(green path)**. Then sew
through a round and an 11º **(red path)**.
Repeat this step around the component.
After making the last picot, just sew
through a round **(gray path)**.

make the base

1. Sew through three 11ºs in the picot
(figure 2, orange path).
2. Pick up three 15º seed beads, and sew
through the middle outer 11º in the next
picot. Repeat around the component.
Don't pull the beads tight **(green path)**.

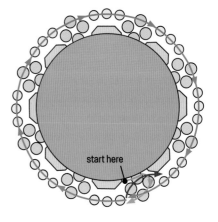

figure 2

3. Place the rivoli inside the component,
face up. The three 15ºs and an 11º will
lie on top of the rivoli. Sew back through
the circle beads a few times, pulling tight
to secure the rivoli in place.
4. Sew down through the next two
11ºs to exit a middle 11º in the base
(blue path).

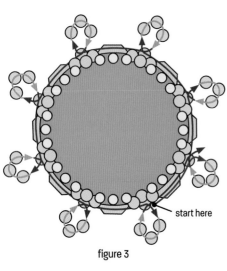

figure 3

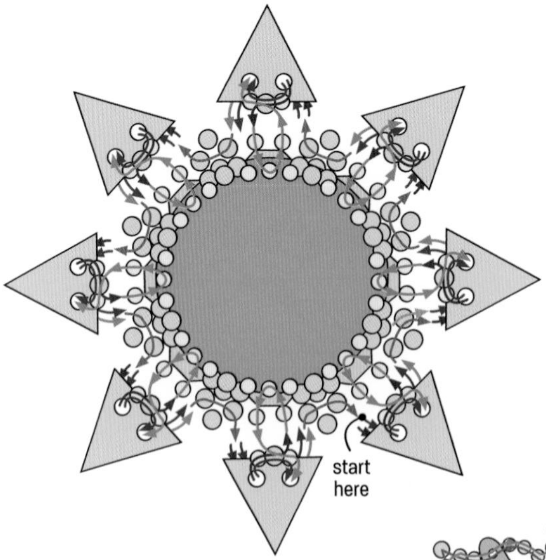

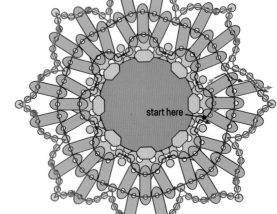

figure 4

figure 5

make the base picots

1. Sew through a round and the next middle 11º in the base picot (**figure 3, red path**).

2. Pick up three 11ºs (**orange path**). Sew back through the 11º in the same direction, a round, and the next middle 11º in the base picot (**blue path**).

3. Repeat step 2 around the component, exiting an 11º. Then sew through a side 11º in the base picot.

add the Triangles

NOTE: In each step, make sure all the beads are snug.

1. Pick up a Triangle (right hole, back to front), a 15º, an 11º, and a 15º, and sew through the same Triangle (left hole, front to back) (**figure 4, red path**).

2. Sew down through the next 11º in the picot and sew up through the next 11º in the picot (**pink path**). Snug the Triangle close to the component so it is laying on top of the round (the Triangle will want to fall to the side, which is OK, as long as you have it snug).

3. Repeat steps 1 and 2 around the component to add the Triangles (the Triangles will fall to the side).

4. Sew through a Triangle (right side, back to front), a 15º, and an 11º (**blue path**).

5. Pick up a 15º, and sew through the middle 15º on top of the rivoli. Pick up a 15º, and sew back through the 11º in the same direction, a 15º, and Triangle (left hole, front to back) (**green path**).

6. With a tight tension, sew down through the next side 11º in the picot and sew up through the next 11º in the picot (**pink path**). At this point the Triangle should not fall to the side, but sit straight out.

7. Repeat steps 4–6 around the component, exiting a side 11º in the picot.

work on the back

1. Flip the pendant over. Exit an 11º, pick up three SuperDuos, and sew down through an 11º and up through an 11º. Repeat around the pendant (**figure 5, blue path**).

2. Exit an 11º, and sew through the three SuperDuos (**orange path**).

3. Sew up through the same SuperDuo (empty hole), pick up a SuperDuo, and sew through a SuperDuo (empty hole). Pick up a SuperDuo, sew through a SuperDuo (empty hole), and pick up an 11º. Repeat around the pendant. When you pick up the last 11º in the step, sew through the next SuperDuo (outside hole) (**red path**).

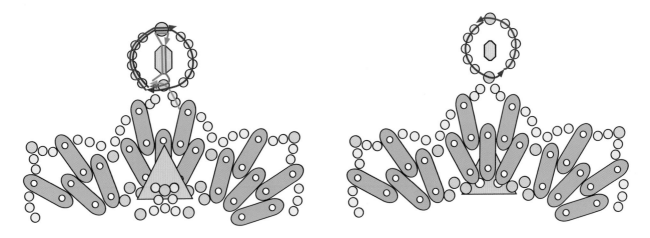

figure 6

figure 8

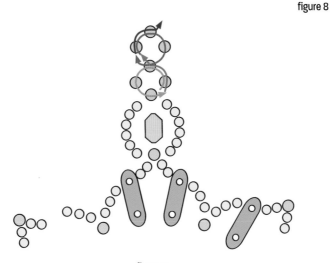

figure 7

4. Sew up through the next SuperDuo (empty hole), pick up two 15ºs, an 11º, and two 15ºs, and sew through the next SuperDuo (empty hole). Pick up three 15ºs, and sew through an 11º. Pick up three 15ºs, and sew through the next SuperDuo (empty hole). Repeat around the pendant (**pink path**).

5. Sew back through the last round of beads, skipping the 11ºs (you may have to pull the 11ºs out with your needle on the outer edge beads to help them lay on top of the 15ºs) (**green path**).

add the bail

1. Flip the pendant over so the front is facing you. Sew through the beadwork to exit an 11º on the edge (**figure 6, orange path**).

2. Pick up a round and an 11º (**green path**). Sew back through the round and the original 11º in the same direction (**pink path**).

3. Pick up six 15ºs, sew through the 11º above the round, pick up six 15ºs, and sew through the 11º below the round (**blue path**).

4. Sew through back through six 15ºs and an 11º (**red path**).

continue the bail

1. Pick up three 11ºs, and sew back through the 11º in the same direction (**figure 7, orange path**).

2. Sew through two 11ºs (**green path**). Pick up three 11ºs, and sew back through the 11º in the same direction (**pink path**). Sew through two 11ºs (**red path**).

finish the back

1. Fold the bail in half, and exit an 11º on the end. Pick up five 15ºs, and sew through the 15º below the round where you started the bail in the same direction. You are creating a circle behind the round (**figure 8, blue path**).

2. Exit an 11º below the round, pick up five 15ºs, and sew back through the 11º you originally exited in the same direction (**red path**). Retrace the thread path, and end the threads (Techniques).

5 other shaped beads

sweet pea
necklace

Enjoy making this pretty necklace with Piggy beads. These unusual beads are slightly cupped, so my design displays them from the side.

supplies

Necklace, 17 in. (43cm)

- **52** Piggy beads
- **50** 4mm pearls or bicones
- 10g 11º seed beads
- 12g SuperDuos
- lobster claw clasp
- 2 in. (5cm) cable chain
- **2** 5mmm jump rings
- 3 in. (7.6cm) chain extender (optional)
- stop bead
- Fireline, 6-lb. test
- beading needle, size 11

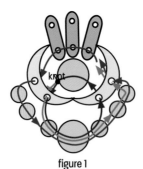

figure 1

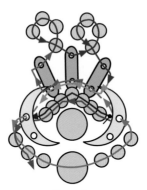

figure 2

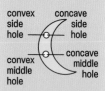

convex side hole — concave side hole — convex middle hole — concave middle hole

WORKING WITH PIGGY BEADS

Piggy beads are circular and have two holes. Lay the beads out on the beading mat all facing the same direction. The instructions will indicate which hole to sew through: concave side, concave middle, convex side, or convex middle.

make the components

NOTE: You will be making a total of 25 components.

1. Thread a needle on 18 in. (46cm) of thread, leaving a 4-in. (10cm) tail. Keep a very tight tension as you stitch. Pick up a Piggy bead (concave side hole), an 11º seed bead, a 4mm pearl, an 11º, a Piggy (convex side hole), and a pearl, and make a circle by sewing back through all the beads again. Tie a surgeon's knot (Techniques, p. 9) **(figure 1, blue path)**.

2. Sew through a Piggy (concave side hole), an 11º, a pearl, and an 11º. Pick up two 11ºs, and sew through a Piggy (convex middle bead) **(green path)**.

3. Pick up three SuperDuos (these SuperDuos will lie behind the pearl), sew through a Piggy (concave middle hole), pick up two 11ºs, and sew through an 11º, a pearl, three 11ºs, and a Piggy (convex middle hole) **(red path)**.

continue

NOTE: Keep a tight tension as you stitch.

1. Pick up seven 11ºs (these 11ºs will lie on top of the SuperDuos) **(figure 2, blue path)**. Sew through a Piggy (concave middle hole), three 11ºs, a pearl, three 11ºs, and a Piggy (convex middle hole) **(green path)**.

2. Sew through three SuperDuos, then sew up through the last SuperDuo again (empty hole) **(pink path)**.

3. Pick up four 11ºs, and sew back through the first 11º picked up in the same direction to make a picot (Techniuqes). Continue through the next Super-Duo (empty hole), and snug the picot between the SuperDuos. Repeat this step **(red path)**.

4. Sew down through the same Super-Duo hole and the next two SuperDuos **(orange path)**.

5. Sew through a Piggy (concave middle hole), three 11ºs, a pearl, three 11ºs, and a Piggy (convex middle hole) **(green path)**.

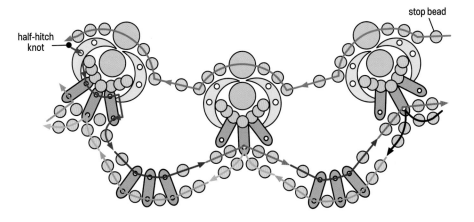

figure 3

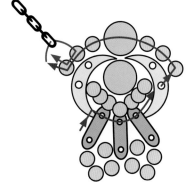

figure 4

6. Sew through three 11ºs, skip an 11º, sew through three 11ºs and a Piggy (concave middle hole), and tie a half-hitch knot (Techniques). Sew through two 11ºs **(gray path)**. End the threads. Repeat both sections to make a total of 25 components.

connect the components

1. Cut a new thread about 1½ yd. (1.4m) long. Add a stop bead (Techniques) and leave about a 6-in. (15cm) tail to add the clasp.

2. Pick up a component, front facing you, by sewing through the top three 11ºs, pearl, and three 11ºs. Pick up an 11º, and sew through the following three 11ºs, pearl, and three 11ºs on another component **(figure 3, green path)**. Repeat to connect all the components together (they will be very loose and wonky at this point).

3. When you have added all the components, pull them together so the 11ºs are snug. Tie a half-hitch knot between an 11º and a Piggy.

4. Sew through the following Piggy (convex middle hole), three SuperDuos, the other hole of the last SuperDuo, and an 11º **(red path)**.

NOTE: In step 5, you will not always be adding a set of three SuperDuos all the way across the necklace. Refer to step 7 for the sequence needed to place the correct number of SuperDuos as you add them across the necklace. This will help give a nice curve to the piece.

5. Pick up an 11º, three SuperDuos, and an 11º **(blue path)**.

6. Sew through the following beads in the next component: two 11ºs (in the picot), a SuperDuo, and two 11ºs (in the picot) **(pink path)**.

7. Repeat steps 5 and 6 until you have reached the other end of the necklace by using the following sequence below: Make a set of three SuperDuos eight times (including the first set you just completed), then a set of four SuperDuos one time, then a set of three SuperDuos six times, then a set of four SuperDuos one time, then a set of three SuperDuos eight times to the end of the necklace.

8. Exit the two 11ºs in a picot at the end of the necklace, and sew through two 11ºs in the picot, a SuperDuo, and two 11ºs in the picot **(black path)**.

9. Pick up two 11ºs, sew through a SuperDuo (empty hole), pick up an 11º, and sew through a SuperDuo (empty hole). Pick up an 11º, and sew through a SuperDuo (empty hole) (adjust accordingly for the four SuperDuos). Pick up two 11ºs **(orange path)**.

10. Sew through two 11ºs in the picot, a SuperDuo and two 11ºs in the picot **(teal path)**.

11. Repeat steps 9 and 10 until you reach the other end of the necklace.

12. Sew through the next 11º in the picot and SuperDuo **(gray path)**.

add the chain and clasp

1. Sew up through the SuperDuo you are exiting and the next two SuperDuos, a Piggy (concave middle hole), three 11ºs, a pearl, and three 11ºs **(figure 4, blue path)**.

2. Sew through the end link of the chain and two 11ºs **(red path)**. Retrace the thread path to to secure the connection.

3. Sew through back through a few beads in the last component, and end the thread (Techniques).

4. Repeat steps 1–3 at the other end of the necklace: Remove the stop bead, and use the existing thread to connect the chain.

moon flower bracelet

Crescent beads are flat like a moon. Two holes run through the center of the shape. I decided to add a little "bling" in the form of crystal montées.

left hole   right hole

WORKING WITH CRESCENT BEADS

Crescent beads are flat and have two holes. Lay all the beads on the beading mat facing the same direction. The instructions will indicate which hole to sew through: left or right.

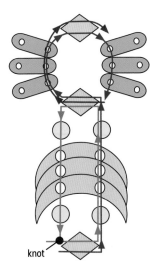

knot

figure 1

supplies
Bracelet, 8 in. (20cm)
- 4g Crescent beads
- 2g MiniDuos
- **25** 3mm bicone crystals
- **12** 3mm Swarovski rose montées
- 3g 15º seed beads
- ball-and-socket clasp
- Fireline, 4-lb. test
- beading needle, size 11

begin the bracelet

1. Thread a needle on 2 yd. (1.8m) of thread, leaving a 4-in. (10cm) tail. Pick up a 3mm crystal, a 15º seed bead, three Crescent beads (right hole), a 15º, a crystal, and a 15º, then sew down through three Crescents (left holes), and pick up a 15º **(figure 1, green path)**. Sew back through all the beads one more time to secure, and tie a surgeon's knot (Techniques, p. 9).

2. Keeping a tight tension, sew back through a crystal, a 15º, three Crescents (right holes), a 15º, and a crystal. Pick up three MiniDuos, a crystal, and three MiniDuos **(red path)**.

3. Sew back through the crystal in the same direction, three MiniDuos, and a crystal **(blue path)**.

add the rose montées

1. Pick up a 3mm rose montée, crystal side up (doesn't matter which hole), and sew through the crystal on the opposite side. Sew back through the rose montée (same hole) and the first crystal in the same direction. Retrace the thread path to secure **(figure 2, green path)**.

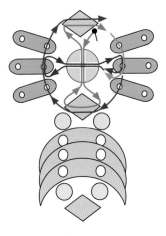

figure 2

2. Sew through two MiniDuos (inside hole) **(figure 2, orange path)**. Sew through a rose montée (empty hole), a MiniDuo (inside hole), the rose montée (same hole), and a MiniDuo (inside hole) in the same direction. Retrace the thread path to secure the rose montée **(figure 2, blue path)**.

3. Sew through a MiniDuo (inside hole), a crystal, three MiniDuos (inside holes), and a crystal **(red path)**. Repeat all of the steps in the project so far, starting by picking up a 15º (and skipping the surgeon's knot) to reach the desired length, leaving room for the clasp. Exit

the last crystal on the end of
the bracelet.

add the clasp and picots

1. Pick up two 15ºs and one half of the
clasp **(figure 3, green path)**. Sew back
through the last 15º, pick up a 15º,
and sew back through the crystal in the
same direction **(blue path)**. Retrace the
thread path to secure the clasp.

2. Sew through the beadwork to exit
the next MiniDuo (empty hole), pick
up three 15ºs, and sew through the
next MiniDuo (empty hole) to make a
picot (Techniques). Pick up three 15ºs,
and sew through the next MiniDuo
(empty hole) **(orange path)**.

3. Repeat step 2 to the end of this side
of the bracelet.

**NOTE: To make the middle 15º point
out, use the needle to pull the
middle 15º away from the bracelet.**

4. Exit the last MiniDuo, and sew
through the following 15º, three
Crescents (right hole), 15º, and crystal
(red path). Repeat steps 1–3 to add the
other half of the clasp and to complete
the other side of the bracelet. End
the threads (Techniques).

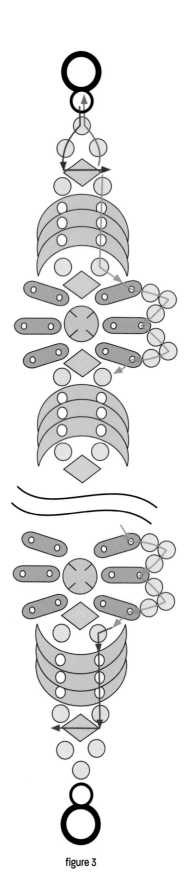

figure 3

crystal diamond earrings

These lovely DiamonDuo beads add a touch of glamour to any piece. The DiamonDuo features a faceted top that catches the light and adds sparkle to a design.

supplies

- **8** DiamonDuo beads
- **16** 3mm bicone crystals
- 3g 15º seed beads
- pair of earring findings
- Fireline, 4-lb. test
- beading needle, size 11

top
hole

bottom
hole

WORKING WITH DIAMONDUO BEADS

DiamonDuo beads have a faceted top and a flat bottom. Lay all the beads out on the beading mat facing the same direction, faceted side facing up. The instructions will indicate which hole to sew through: top or bottom.

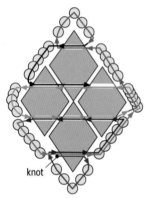
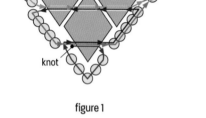

knot

figure 1

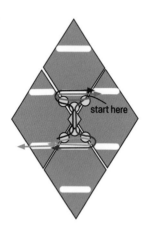

start here

figure 2

begin the earrings

1. Thread a needle on 2 yd. (1.8m) of thread, leaving a 4-in. (10cm) tail. Pick up a DiamonDuo bead (bottom hole, left to right) and five 15º seed beads. Sew back through all the beads, then tie a surgeon's knot (Techniques, p. 9) **(figure 1, red path)**.

2. Sew through the DiamonDuo (bottom hole, left to right), pick up five 15ºs and a DiamonDuo (bottom hole, right to left), and sew through the first DiamonDuo (top hole, right to left). Pick up a DiamonDuo (bottom hole, right to left) **(blue path)**.

3. Pick up five 15ºs, and sew back through the first DiamonDuo (bottom hole, left to right) and five 15ºs **(green path)**.

4. Pick up five 15ºs, and sew through a DiamonDuo (top hole, right to left). Pick up a DiamonDuo (bottom hole, right to left), and sew through the next Diamon-Duo (top hole, right to left). Pick up five 15ºs, and sew through three DiamonDu-os (bottom hole, top hole, then bottom hole, all right to left) **(orange path)**.

5. Sew through five 15ºs, pick up five 15ºs, and sew through a Diamon-Duo (top hole, right to left). Pick up five 15ºs **(pink path)**.

6. Sew back through the DiamonDuo (top hole, right to left), pick up five 15ºs, and sew through two DiamonDuos (top hole, then bottom hole, all right to left) **(black path)**.

add the center crystal

1. Keep a tight tension. Pick up two 15ºs, a crystal, and two 15ºs, and sew down through the adjacent DiamonDuo (top hole, right to left) **(figure 2, red path)**.
2. Pick up a 15º, and sew back up through a 15º, a crystal, and a 15º. Pick up a 15º, and sew through the original DiamonDuo (bottom hole, left to right) **(blue path)**.
3. Sew back through a 15º, skip the 15º above the crystal, and sew through a 15º and a DiamonDuo (bottom hole, left to right). Retrace the thread path **(green path)** to secure the 15ºs.
4. Sew down through two 15ºs, a crystal, two 15ºs, and the lower DiamonDuo (top hole, right to left) **(red path)**.
5. Sew back through a 15º, skip the 15º below the crystal, and sew through the next 15º and DiamonDuo (top hole, right to left). Repeat this step to secure the beads **(pink path)**.
6. Exit a middle DiamonDuo (top hole, right to left), and sew through a DiamonDuo (bottom hole, right to left) **(orange path)**.

make the picots

1. Sew up through three 15ºs, and pick up three 15ºs **(figure 3, blue path)**.
2. Sew through the first 15º in the same direction, and then sew through three 15ºs, and pick up three 15ºs. Repeat this step around the component to complete the picots (Techniques). After you have added the last three 15ºs, sew through the 15º in the same direction and sew through three 15ºs **(red path)**.

finish the earrings

1. Sew through two 15ºs in the base and two 15ºs in the picot, pick up a crystal, and sew through two 15ºs in the picot,

figure 3

two 15ºs in the base, and two 15ºs in the picot **(blue path)**.
2. Pick up four 15ºs, an earring finding, and four 15ºs, and sew through the 15º you exited in the same direction. Retrace the thread path to secure the connection **(orange path)**.
3. Exit the middle 15º in the picot, and sew through a 15º in the picot, two 15ºs on the base, and two 15ºs in the picot. Pick up a crystal, and sew through two 15ºs in the picot, three 15ºs in the base, and two 15ºs in the picot. Pick up a crystal, and sew through two 15ºs in the picot, two 15ºs in the base, and a 15º in the picot **(red path)**.
4. Pick up two 15ºs, a crystal, a 15º, a crystal, and three 15ºs **(green path)**.
5. Sew back through the crystal and 15º, pick up a crystal and two 15ºs, and sew through a 15º in the picot, two 15ºs in the base, and two 15ºs in the picot. Pick up a crystal, and sew through two 15ºs in the picot and two 15ºs in the base **(pink path)**. Sew through a few more beads, tie a half-hitch knot, and end the threads (Techniques).
6. Repeat to make a second earring.

figure 4

faceted
arches
bracelet

This dynamic piece has plenty of dimension, making it perfect for a night out or in. Arcos Par Puca beads are odd-shaped, so be sure to pick up the beads correctly while stitching!

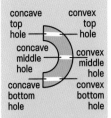

concave top hole — convex top hole
concave middle hole — convex middle hole
concave bottom hole — convex bottom hole

WORKING WITH ARCOS BEADS

Arcos Par Puca beads feature a concave and convex side with a crescent moon shape. Place the beads with the holes in a horizontal direction. The instructions will indicate which hole to sew through: concave or convex top, concave or convex middle, and concave or convex bottom.

start the bracelet

1. Thread a needle on 2 yd. (1.8m) of thread, leaving a 4-in. (10cm) tail. Add a stop bead (Techniques, p. 9). Pick up a 15º seed bead, an Arcos bead (convex middle hole), a 15º, a 6mm round crystal, a 15º, an Arcos (concave middle hole), and a 15º. Repeat for the desired length for the bracelet, leaving room for the clasp **(figure 1, pink path)**.

2. After adding the last 15º, sew back through an Arcos (convex middle hole), a 15º, a round, a 15º, an Arcos (concave middle hole), and a 15º. Repeat until you reach the last 15º **(green path)**.

3. Remove the stop bead, and tie a surgeon's knot with the working thread and tail (Techniques).

4. Sew back through the end 15º, pick up three 15ºs, and sew through an Arcos (convex bottom hole). Pick up two MiniDuos, and sew through an Arcos (concave bottom hole) **(red path)**.

5. Pick up a 15º, a 3mm bicone crystal, and a 15º, and sew through an Arcos (convex bottom hole). Pick up two MiniDuos, and sew through an Arcos (concave bottom hole). Repeat to the end of the bracelet **(blue path)**. Pick up three 15ºs **(gray path)**.

6. Repeat steps 4 and 5 on the other side of the bracelet. Then sew through four 15ºs on the end **(orange path)**.

supplies

Bracelet, 8 in. (20cm)
- 6g Arcos Par Puca beads
- **12** 6mm round crystals (Swarovski)
- **66** 3mm bicone crystals
- 8g MiniDuos
- 5g 15º seed beads
- ball-and-socket clasp
- stop bead
- Fireline, 6-lb. test
- beading needle, size 11

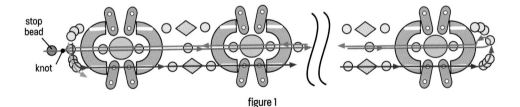

figure 1

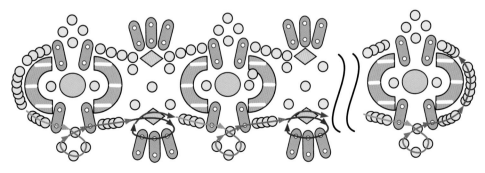

figure 2

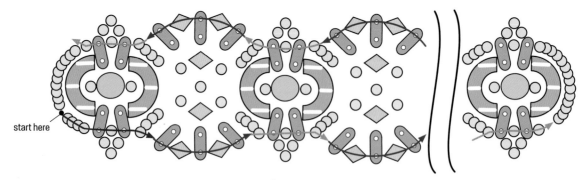

start here

figure 3

embellish the bracelet

1. Pick up four 15ºs, and sew through a MiniDuo (empty hole) (**figure 2, orange path**).

2. Pick up four 15ºs (**green path**). Sew back through the first 15º picked up in the same direction, and continue through a MiniDuo (empty hole). Pick up four 15ºs (**pink path**).

3. Sew through a bicone, and pick up three MiniDuos (**blue path**). Sew back through the bicone in the same direction (**red path**).

4. Repeat steps 1–3 to the end of the bracelet, ending with picking up four 15ºs. Then sew through the seven 15ºs on the end (**gray path**).

5. Repeat steps 1–4 to complete the other side of the bracelet.

finish the bracelet

1. Sew through four 15ºs, a MiniDuo, a 15º, a MiniDuo, and a 15º (**figure 3, blue path**).

2. Sew through a MiniDuo (empty hole), pick up a bicone, and sew through a MiniDuo (empty hole). Pick up a

bicone, and sew through a MiniDuo (empty hole) (**red path**).

3. Sew through a 15º, a MiniDuo, a 15º, a MiniDuo, and a 15º (**orange path**).

4. Repeat steps 2 and 3 to the end of the bracelet.

add the clasp

1. Exit a 15º, and sew through the next eight 15ºs (**figure 4, blue path**).

2. Pick up three 15ºs and one half of the clasp (**orange path**). Sew back through the last 15º, pick up two 15ºs, and sew through the three middle 15ºs in the same direction (**red path**). Retrace the thread path to secure the connection.

3. Sew through six 15ºs, a MiniDuo, a 15º, a MiniDuo, and a 15º (**pink path**).

4. Repeat "Finish the Bracelet" (starting at step 2) through "Add the Clasp" on the other side of the bracelet. End the threads (Techniques).

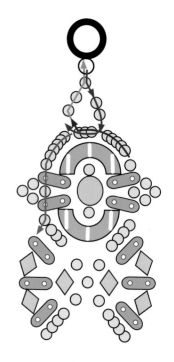

figure 4

hex elegance
earrings

A simple shape makes a big impact in these cool earrings. Made with Hex Pyramid beads, these earring drops are a sight to behold.

top hole
bottom hole

supplies

- **2** Hex Pyramid beads
- **6** 3mm bicone crystals
- **16** 3mm bugle beads
- 1g 15º seed beads
- pair of earring findings
- Fireline, 6-lb. test
- beading needle, size 11

begin the earrings

1. Thread a needle on 1 yd. (.9m) of thread, leaving a 4-in. (10cm) tail. Pick up a Pyramid bead (bottom hole, left to right) and a bugle bead, and sew back through the Pyramid (top hole, right to left). Pick up a bugle. Sew back through all the beads, and tie a surgeon's knot (**figure 1, blue path**).

2. Sew through the Pyramid (bottom hole) and a bugle (**orange path**).

3. Pick up three 15ºs seed beads, a bugle, five 15ºs, a bugle, and three 15ºs, and sew through a bugle. Repeat (**green path**).

4. Sew through three 15ºs, a bugle, and two 15ºs. Skip a 15º, and sew through two 15ºs, a bugle, three 15ºs, a bugle, three 15ºs, a bugle, and two 15ºs. Skip a 15º, and sew through two 15ºs, a bugle, three 15ºs, and a bugle (**green and red paths**).

finish the earrings

1. Sew through three 15ºs and a bugle, and pick up two 15ºs, a bugle, five 15ºs, an earring finding, and four 15ºs (**figure 2, red path**).

2. Sew through the first 15º picked up after the bugle in the same direction, pick up a bugle and two 15ºs, and sew through a bugle, three 15ºs, a bugle,

knot

figure 1

figure 2

three 15ºs, and a bugle (**orange path**).

3. Pick up three 15ºs, a 3mm bicone crystal, three 15ºs, a crystal, and three 15ºs (**blue path**).

4. Sew back through the crystal and the 15º above the crystal, pick up a 15º, and sew back through the 15º below the first crystal. Pick up a crystal and three 15ºs, and sew through a bugle, three 15ºs, and a bugle (**green path**). Repeat steps 1–4 by sewing through all the beads to secure and to give the earring a nice shape. End the thread (Techniques).

5. Repeat to make a second earring.

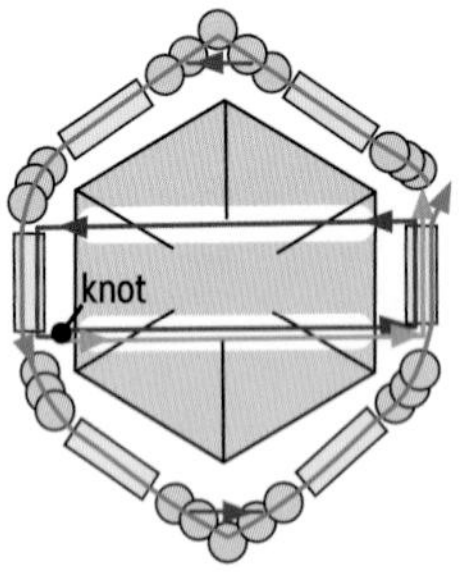

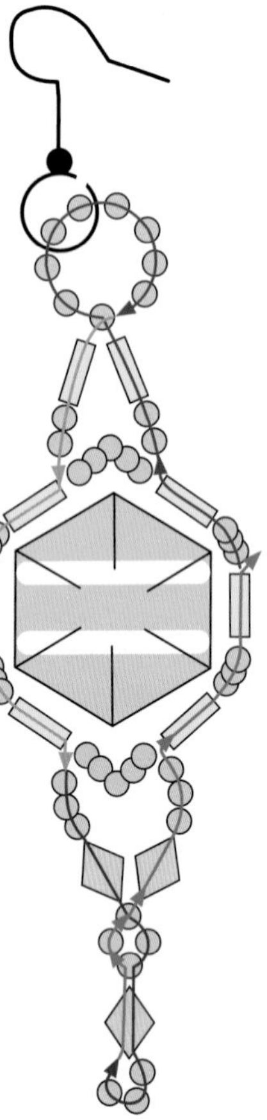

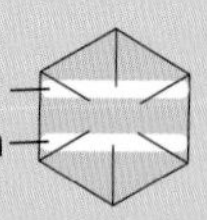

WORKING WITH HEX PYRAMID BEADS

Hex Pyramid beads have a pointed top and flat bottom. The illustrations show a flat bead. Place the beads on your beading mat with the pointed side up and with the holes in a horizontal direction. The instructions will indicate which hole to sew through: top or bottom.

acknowledgments

I would like to thank Erica and Dianne at Kalmbach for all your help, advice, and encouragement, along with all the other Kalmbach staff that helped to make this book a dream come true. A big thank you to Shannon, the owner at Meant to Bead, for helping and encouraging me to discover my full protentional as a designer and teacher. Thank you to all my family, friends, and students for being there for me, encouraging me, and inspiring me as a designer and a teacher. Special thanks to my wonderful husband, Jerry—I could have not done this without you—for supporting me and being my biggest cheerleader! Most of all, I would like to thank my Lord and Savior. Without Him, I could have never done this; He is the one who created me to be creative, to be a teacher and a designer. And most of all, He made this all possible!

about the author

Five years ago, Renee and her husband moved to Appleton, Wisconsin, from Milwaukee. When they moved to Appleton, Renee just had to go and find all the beading stores in and around her area. One day, out of the blue, she was asked if she would be interested in teaching at a local bead store. She tried it and loved it! Well, the next thing she knew, she was designing and teaching her very own designs. In 2014, Renee started an Etsy shop, ElegancebyRenee (etsy.com/shop/ElegancebyRenee), where she has been selling her patterns ever since. The last few years, she has been teaching her designs at a few wonderful beading stores throughout Wisconsin, as well as the Madison Art Glass & Bead show in Madison, Wisconsin.

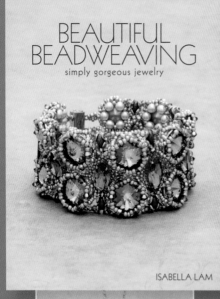
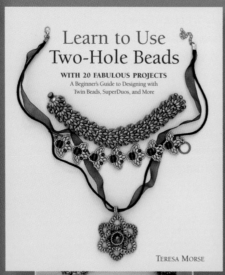
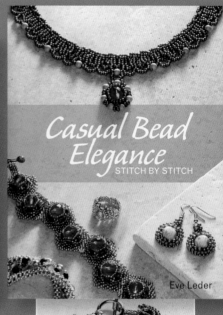